Love in a Time of Fear

Love in a Time of Fear

Hearing Our Neighbors Across Lines that Divide Us

CASSIE J. E. H. TRENTAZ

WIPF & STOCK · Eugene, Oregon

LOVE IN A TIME OF FEAR
Hearing Our Neighbors Across Lines that Divide Us

Wipf & Stock
An Imprint of Wipf and Stock Publishers
199 W. 8th Ave., Suite 3
Eugene, OR 97401

www.wipfandstock.com

PAPERBACK ISBN: 978-1-5326-3538-0
HARDCOVER ISBN: 978-1-5326-3540-3
EBOOK ISBN: 978-1-5326-3539-7

Manufactured in the U.S.A.   08/28/18

For my students. You are also my teachers.

And for Jason and Angel who inspire me to work as hard as I humanly can.

You are loved. You are not alone.

Contents

Introduction

Three Quick Stories and All We Need to Start

STORY ONE

My son Winston is allergic to peanuts. We found out through a terrifying experience of watching his little body respond to something that it was convinced was toxic to him. Things began to swell. We sprang into action. Thankfully, when the experience was over, my son was fine. We acted rapidly and he recovered. We also had a crucial new piece of information about him.

I didn't know Winston was allergic to peanuts when I gave them to him. How could I know? No one else in our family is allergic to peanuts. But that didn't mean that the allergy wasn't real. The response of his body told me quickly enough that it was.

I wasn't angry with Winston for the fact that his body rejected the peanuts I gave him. I didn't try to convince him otherwise. In that moment, I wanted nothing more than to make the wrong right and re-secure his health and safety. I love my son. And one way that I show him that love now is by making sure that peanuts stay far, far away from him.

This story is true for Winston. It can also be a metaphor for the content of this book.

We are not all the same. The ways we walk in the world are not all the same. What harms us is not all the same. What brings us joy is not all the same. We cannot always predict what will cause harm or what will bring care to people whose experiences are very different from our own. We are not the experts on their experiences. They are. It did not make me a terrible mother for not knowing ahead of time that my son was allergic to peanuts.

Sometimes you don't know until you know. However, we might raise some significant questions if I continue to give him peanuts without regard for the fact that his body has told us that they are toxic to him.

Many people I know, myself included, do not really like being wrong. Most people I know, myself included, do not like hurting other people. But sometimes we are. And sometimes we do. And in those moments, we have crucial decisions to make. Do we hold to the ideas we have that others tell us are harmful or do we open ourselves to something new? Do we deny that we are responsible for any pain caused or accept that we hurt someone and figure out how to move forward from there? Do we learn? Do we defend? Can we do both?

STORY TWO

Here's another example. The other day, while driving to work, I went to change lanes. The problem was, there was a car already there. We saw each other in time to avoid the accident. But in the interchange, I had become hyper-aware that someone was there when I had not previously noticed them. I had some decisions to make.

I did not mean to take up someone else's space on the road. I simply hadn't seen them. The car was in my blind spot, something all cars have. I didn't mean harm and a lot of harm was averted, but I had taken an action that could have caused harm and only didn't because the other car was vigilant and helped me to avoid further damage. Maybe the person in the other car is used to this sort of thing. Maybe it happens far too often.

So what do I do when I realize what happened? Do I blame the other car for being where I couldn't see them? Do I recognize my blind spot and take responsibility? Do I look more closely next time, realizing that I still might make mistakes in the future, but work to keep reducing those? Do I say a little prayer of thanks for the other driver who was paying attention and vow to not make that their responsibility next time?

I grew up in a small town in the Kansas heartland surrounded by big skies and wheat fields and people who work hard and pray hard and strive diligently to take care of each other. That description is apt for my family as much as it is for the entire community. My dad is a retired military Lieutenant Colonel who was also a favorite sixth grade science teacher and elementary school principal. My mom is a retired masterful kindergarten teacher, beloved storyteller at the library story hour, and caregiver. Both are staples in our small community and model the deep roots of community and faith that mark the culture of that part of our world. This upbringing has given me incredibly important values that are applicable across contexts.

And the reality remains that the places where I have lived away from that community where I grew up—a blue collar factory town in Indiana, the south side of the sprawling (and often racially charged) city of Chicago, and now in a bustling urban environment in the Pacific Northwest—have been very different from the context of my growing up. This is not a statement of better or worse. It is a statement of difference and learning.

The faith of my family and my community growing up held and holds to a foundational love of God and neighbor. And what I have learned, which may seem obvious, but has needed to be stated in my own life, is that my neighbors are different in different contexts. My neighbors' experiences and lives are different. In order to love my neighbors, I have needed to get to know those stories and those realities of my real neighbors and not simply map onto them what I learned growing up, which were often things that do not fit their realities. That does not mean what I learned growing up isn't important or that there aren't significant truths to it. It does mean that those truths have been partial and not complete. I knew important pieces of the world growing up. I did not know the whole. I still don't.

It did not make me a terrible mother for not knowing ahead of time that my son was allergic to peanuts.

I legitimately didn't see the other person in my blind spot when I began to move into a lane not previously my own. (Why is my blind spot there and how did it get there, anyway?)

But when I did realize what happened, the crucial moment was in what happened next. How did, how will I respond?

We live in a connected world, now more so than ever. Our connections to one another through policies and voting, through connections via the world wide web and our phones and computers, through business practices and trade, mean that, regardless of whether we live in a small rural community in the heartland, or a large coastal urban city, our tables need to both deepen and expand. The people on our minds and hearts need to deepen and expand. Our concept of neighbor needs to deepen and expand. My hope is that this book can help.

ALL WE NEED TO START

> "We are all the needy and the ones who meet needs. To place our-
> selves or anyone else in only one category is to lie to ourselves."[1]

On the surface, I am a white, middle-class, straight, US-born, woman trying to follow the way of Jesus. For people who are like me in any of those
categories, this book is both about us and not about us. This book will give
us access to stories of amazing people and communities to whom we are often outsiders. This book will tell about experiences that may seem familiar
or may seem very distant from our own. The point is not to find ourselves
in these stories. This book is not about us.

But this book is also directly about us. In reading, in listening to the
stories and experiences shared here, we will have decisions to make. It will
be our job to figure out how to receive these stories and to recognize what
happens within us. Where and why do we feel moved? Where and why we
do feel defensive? Where and why do we feel inspired? Where and why do
we feel outraged? Where and why do we feel responsible? Where and why
do we care?

It will also be our job to figure out what do with these insights. Luckily, the amazing people who offer their voices and stories in this text give
us many handles for how to move forward. I will articulate those suggestions in their own words and via summaries throughout as well as in the
concluding chapter.

We do not need to know everything already before we start this book.
All that we absolutely need to begin is a spirit of curiosity and an openness
to the possibility of learning something new. As my friend Leroy Barber
puts it, "Let people surprise you. Put your biases away and let people introduce themselves on their terms."[2]

Almost none of us find ourselves in all of the identity categories explored here. In that sense, we can relax knowing that we all have much to
learn. All of us have absorbed certain messages about at least some of the
communities highlighted in this book. So, I ask that you simply approach
the stories with a willingness to hear, to identify your own questions, to
think about your own experiences, and to be willing to consider both how
yours are similar and how yours are different from the neighbors' stories
presented here. I ask, out of a spirit of curiosity, that you try to take the

---

1. Bolz-Weber, *Accidental Saints,* 48.
2. Barber, *Embrace,* 66.

initial posture of respecting or honoring rather than analyzing at first.[3] The neighbors we hear from will help us learn how to do that even better.

Some of us will receive what is in these pages readily with open hands. Some of us may have to take things bit by bit. Some of us may have to calm our "fix-it" jumping beans down in order to hear and let things soak in more deeply. All of that is welcome here. Enter as you enter. I only ask that you do so with a spirit of curiosity and the willingness to make a little more room at your table as you listen and process what it all means.

EXCURSUS: ANOTHER WORD ABOUT MY OWN IDENTITY

Earlier, I identified myself as a white, middle-class, straight, US-born woman trying to follow the way of Jesus. Those identity markers set me apart from every single one of the communities and voices highlighted in this text in at least one way. As such, that could raise questions regarding appropriation of others' stories and assuming others' voices to serve agendas and purposes different from their own. I am aware of this concern and this oft-enacted reality. They are important and legitimate questions to ask: Why me? Why am I writing this book? And why am I, specifically, the one writing this book?

In one sense, I answer the "why me" questions by saying that I am writing this book because the communities highlighted in this book are four communities that I care deeply about and who are experiencing significant amounts of pressures and often discrimination in our world today. They are communities that I have spent years trying to listen to, learn from, and figure out how to show support and care to in ways that they receive as support and care. They are also communities that were largely absent from the community that I grew up in, communities that I wish someone had introduced me to earlier.

But my voice is not a substitute for the voices of those most directly impacted. Recognizing this, I have worked to highlight the voices of the communities whose stories are told here as much as possible in their own words. As such, I am writing this book as a bit of a bridge to introduce people that I care about to other people that I care about and who are often separated by geography, politics, and/or religion. Let this only be a

---

3. Ibid.

beginning and not a replacement for hearing more stories of others in their own voices. This book, too, is partial. This, too, is a beginning.

PART I

Setting the Context

"The most important one," answered Jesus, "is this: 'Hear, O Israel: The Lord our God, the Lord is one. Love the Lord your God with all your heart and with all your soul and with all your mind and with all your strength.' The second is this. 'Love your neighbor as yourself.' There is no commandment greater than these," (Mark 12:29–31).

"An enemy is a person whose story we have not heard."[1]

---

1. Hoffman, "An Enemy is One."

1

1

On Love and Fear When the Whole World is on Fire

THE WHOLE WORLD IS ON FIRE

LAST YEAR SOME TEENAGERS playing with fireworks ignited a wildfire that jumped the Columbia River, burned significant parts of the river gorge, and threatened the outer edges of our city. Ash covered our cars like snow. The sun looked pink through the smoke.

A few weeks later, the most destructive wildfire in the history of California destroyed significant parts of the area around and within Santa Rosa. Other fires burned up and down the Western coast. Grassfires in the dry and windy heartland ripped through farm and ranch lands with ferocity. It seemed like everyone was watching their social media feeds for news of "containment" and a chance to breathe again. It felt at times that the whole world was on fire.

And political fires have raged just as fiercely. I am writing this book during 2017–2018 in the currently hotly divided United States of America. For many, it feels like the whole world is still on fire.

For most people I know, the 2016 Presidential election was a difficult one. For some, the choice itself was not difficult as they sided clearly with one candidate or the other (or neither), but the tone and tenor of the campaign was difficult. For others, the choice itself was difficult. Neither candidate seemed like a good fit. They were unsatisfied. I heard a lot of, "I'm

3

afraid *if this happens* then *this will happen* statements. Fear seemed to be ever-present, often even in the driver's seat.

Many people I know wrestled with knowing what would be best for their families and struggled knowing that perhaps the answer to that question might conflict with what is best for others. Others went with a clear sense of what they thought was best for their families and were somewhat shocked that so much of the country seemed to be on the "other side." When the people around our tables are mostly like us that sometimes happens. When our contexts are so different from one another that sometimes happens.

I watched the 2016 US presidential election unfold, as did many of my friends, neighbors, and family, with great interest. It felt like a lot was at stake. We weren't wrong. And what felt at stake for me was sometimes different than what felt at stake for my family and friends. What wasn't different was how passionately we felt it. That passion was not simply for our candidate but, often, fear of what might happen if the other candidate won. Now the results are in. We have been living with them for two years. The folks on one side of the spectrum have rejoiced at times (although sometimes only kind of) while the folks on the other side have erupted in anger, grief, fear, and questions about what this means for our lives now. The election and its aftermath revealed and reminded us of significant divisions that exist in our nation today. They did not necessarily create them; they simply brought them to the surface.

This election brought out divisions between rural spaces and cities. It demonstrated those among generations. It showed us divisions among classes, races, and genders. It illustrated them between citizens and immigrants. It has ignited fear and grief among many of the communities who were targets of harmful language throughout the election season, among them immigrant and refugee communities, Muslim Americans, LGBTQ+[1] communities, and African American youth. For them, this seems to be another affront in a long line of friction and marginalization. Likewise, it has ignited confusion among people in other communities as to why so many people are so grieved and angry. Disconnects are rampant. With them come confusion and fear.

1. LGBTQ+ is shorthand for the Lesbian, Gay, Bisexual, Transgender, and Queer community. It also includes a + recognizing that human sexuality, sexual identity, and sexual expression go even beyond these identities. Another term that also sometimes serves as shorthand representing people in this community is GSM for Gender and Sexual Minorities.

This is true even within groups that are supposed to hold things in common. Up to 81 percent of white Evangelical Christians voted for the candidate who won.[2] This was by far the largest group voting for the Trump administration. By contrast, Trump received the "lowest minority vote in decades," demonstrated by only 8 percent of the African American vote, including those who also have strong identity within the Christian faith.[3] How is it that people of the same faith tradition can be so strongly split down political lines?

We do not all experience the world the same.

TURNING UP THE HEAT

Differences are real. As a teacher, I make it a practice to invite guests into my classrooms so that students can benefit from different perspectives and have access to some amazing people and ideas. Sometimes I select specific people in order to create moments that turn the heat up just a little bit to see how the group responds and to begin getting us thinking about crucial questions that will be important in our learning. Sometimes this is strategic and I am ready for it. I learn a lot about my students in those moments. Sometimes, however, the heat turns on even when I did not expect it. Last fall I had one of those kinds of experiences.

I invited my friend Leroy Barber to come into class to talk about his work and approach to community development and engagement as well as recent work in Houston where he participated in relief efforts for those impacted by Hurricane Harvey. He also had just been in Dallas where he took part in an action as part of a wider movement called #NFLkneeldown calling out the NFL and the US for continuing to operate in systemically unjust ways toward people of color. Things got political quick.

As with most college classrooms, my students come from a wide spectrum of political orientations. A few particular statements from Leroy ignited one of my students who quickly and thickly engaged. Leroy engaged back. The student continued. The exchange was dialed in, carried a kind of intensity that political conversations sometimes do, and yet was not overtly disrespectful. I watched and listened intently, but even more so, I was watching the body language of everyone else in the room. Our

2. Smith and Martínez, "How the Faithful Voted."
3. Eiser, "Trump Won with the Lowest Minority Vote."

faces and our bodies tell a lot about how comfortable we are in moments of potential conflict, even if it is not directly pointed at or involving us.

Then, the conversation took a turn. My student brought up one particularly charged topic and the rest of the class sprung to life around the circle like a bag of popcorn kernels that had reached their popping heat. One student walked out. Several students' blood pressures visibly escalated as they wriggled in their seats, jaws tensing, but they did not say a word. I took the opportunity to use my voice in that moment to recognize what had been said, some of the responses that it brought, and to make room for some other voices in the room that had not been speaking, and, as we were nearing the end of class time, to take a pause to speak gratitude to Leroy for his presence and contributions. Many students expressed gratitude for things Leroy said. He removed some of their aloneness. He made them think about things they hadn't before. Some of them could not look each other in the eyes, at least not at that moment. Things were not resolved. They were stirred up. Then class ended.

This is not an unusual scenario. In many ways, it is indicative of the climate within which we are living. Life is simply not the same for all of us. We experience things differently based on our identities, where we live, what we have been through, what we believe, how directly impacted we are by whichever topic or policy or question is at hand. If we want to, we can find a place where we can shout our perspectives and then leave. We can find places where we can find others to affirm our perspectives. We can also find places where others will let us know quite boldly that ours is not the only perspective on the planet.

Ours is the era of Charlottesville, Ferguson, Standing Rock, Dallas, Flint, Orlando, and Charleston. It is the era of high stakes debates regarding immigration, health care, terrorism, gun control, climate concerns, and sexual assault. It is an era when we are asking whose lives matter and to whom. Ours is the Obama to post-Obama to Trump era of politics. For many, it feels like all bets are off. For some, it feels like that is how it has been for a long time now.

Ours is an era when so many of us have a deep-rooted anxiety. We feel it even if we can't always name it. We know deep down that there are things and people that we don't understand and we feel, perhaps in the very same deep places, that others don't understand us. Ours is an era marked by great harm and great grief, great misunderstanding, and significant fear.

It is also an era marked by beautiful and powerful examples of people jumping into the fray with hope and compassion, reaching across the lines that divide us and working together to heal our world and ourselves. This book intends to be a piece of that healing work by choosing to not look away from that anxiety or pretend it isn't there but to help us understand ourselves and each other a little bit more. As such, this book will stare these divisions right in the eyes and ask the questions: What is going on? What does it look like to know and love our very different neighbors? What does it look like to be a little bit less afraid and a little bit more connected?

ON FEAR

> "Do not be afraid . . . Among all the things the church has to say to the world today, this may be the most important."[4]

In a de-escalation training last year, one of the first exercises our facilitator asked us to do was to tell a partner a moment when we felt afraid. It was not hard for me to come up with a story. When given the prompt, I immediately thought about the time when my then two year old son let himself out the front door and went on a walk, unbeknownst to my husband and me.

Perry and I were finishing a quick conversation when Winston said he wanted a snack and walked out of the room around the corner. I told him I'd be right there. No more than five minutes later, I made good on my promise, walked around the corner to make Winston his snack, and found the locks undone and the front door open. I have never known such a whole body gripping terror than I experienced upon discovering he was gone.

I shouted up to Perry that Winston was gone and ran out the door, barefoot, five months pregnant with our daughter, and in a split-second decided to run the direction toward both the park and a four-lane heavily trafficked road. As I ran, I scanned the park for a tiny bright green shirt. There was none. And as I ran past the park toward the busy road, I repeated over and over "Oh God please." Fear was my dominant trait in that moment. It ran my whole existence.

Arriving at the road a moment later, I turned the corner to see two cars stopped on my side of the road. My heart stopped with them, unsure for a fleeting second what had brought them to that stop and whether or

4. Bader-Saye, *Following Jesus*, 11.

not it was "too late." But there, on the sidewalk next to the cars, standing and breathing, in one-whole piece, was my little boy in a bright green shirt talking to two stranger-neighbors who had rightly stopped at the sight of a two-year-old walking alone down the sidewalk. They were the owners of the first vehicle. The second vehicle, with two grandmotherly women, had stopped to observe the first vehicle and help if needed or make sure no funny business went down. Everyone looked up when I huffed around the corner.

"I'm going this way," I heard Winston tell the woman kneeling to talk to him as he pointed the direction away from our home. She looked appropriately frazzled.

I approached. Quickly. On a mission. Soaked clear through with fresh terror and relief.

"Hi, Mamma," tiny Winston said, smiling at the sight of me. Smiles were not what I received from the woman who had stopped to help him. She quickly gave me a lecture on parenting, clearly shaken herself by the experience we had all just had. I thanked her flatly unable to muster the energy to care about anything other than the fact that Winston was safe. He was back in my arms. There had been no guarantee that that was going to be the outcome. It felt like pure grace of a second chance. And it wasn't until the cars drove away and Winston and I turned the corner toward home, that I began to sob.

Winston did not want to talk about that day for a while. Neither did I, frankly, but I double-checked every lock on every door and barely let him out of my sight for a very long time.

Why We Fear

Fear sears. It scores us. It shapes us. It determines our behaviors. Sometimes it keeps us safe or it helps us keep others safe. Sometimes it comes because we were not able to keep ourselves or someone else safe in the past and we do not want to live that again. Fear is primal. It is instinctive. It is one of those "reptilian brain" mechanisms that propels us to act or react to the circumstances around and within us. When we are afraid, we are not thinking; we are reacting. So what happens when fear is a dominant characteristic of the time and place in which we live?

At times fear is a gift. It can show us when things are out of whack or downright dangerous. However, problems arise when fear is directed in ways or in volumes that are not helpful or necessary or that are simply counter-productive. We are creatures of instinct but not only creatures of instinct. We are also social-cultural-communal creatures. Our fear mechanism is wired into us instinctually, but the content or object of those fears is socially constructed. Our bodies know how to fear, but we learn what and when and who to fear through experiences as well as by the values and images we absorb in the culture or society within which we live.[5]

Fear can motivate. It can also destabilize. When we are afraid, we are not always in control. This creates the potential that fears can be used to move us to act how particular figures or companies or governments or religions or <u>fill in the blank</u> want us to act. Fear moves us to buy certain things. It moves us to vote certain ways. Fear moves us to open or close our doors and our mouths, our hearts and our homes. Fear shapes how we view the world. It shapes how we act in it.

Sometimes fear can go awry. Medieval theologian Thomas Aquinas asserts that fear can go awry in two major ways. "We can fear *what* we should not . . . Or we can fear *as* we should not." In other words, our fear is out of whack if what we fear is not actually a "great or imminent" threat to us or the people we love. And our fear is out of whack if the amount of fear that we feel toward something or someone is greater than the actual potential danger.[6] Fear can be misplaced. And/or fear can be excessive. When either of these is true, we risk damage to us and to those around us. And studies show that for US Americans, our fears are on the rise.

What We Fear

In the Chapman University Survey of American Fears, US Americans state their list of what they feared most in 2017. You can find the list of the top fears on their website. You can also see how they have changed since 2016.[7] However, what I find especially interesting is not necessarily that the particular fears have changed, but that a higher percentage of people are afraid of those things. Fear is on the rise. When I think about the fear that I often see show up in moments as contentious as ours, there are at least three big categories beyond or below those particulars that impact the stories in this

---

5. Ibid., 25.

6. Qtd. in Bader-Saye, *Following Jesus,* 53.

7. Chapman University, "America's Top Fears 2017."

book: fear of the unknown or uncertain, fear of being wrong, and fear of insecurity. Often all three are wrapped up together.

Fear of the Unknown

In a commencement speech to a group of brand-new college graduates, David Foster Wallace unpacks the "liberal arts mantra" of "teaching people how to think." In his salty and direct way, he calls them and us to question our notions of certainty, declaring to these grads that "a huge percentage of the stuff that I tend to be automatically certain of is, it turns out, totally wrong and deluded."[8]

This is not a statement to shame. It is also not primarily about simply being wrong. It is a statement recognizing the reality that all of our truths are partial and all filtered through the perceived certainty of our own experiences, thoughts, and senses. Wallace continues:

> Here's one example of the utter wrongness of something I tend to be automatically sure of. Everything in my own immediate experience supports my deep belief that I am the absolute center of the universe, the realest, most vivid and important person in existence. We rarely think about this sort of natural, basic self-centeredness, because it's so socially repulsive, but it's pretty much the same for all of us, deep down. It is our default setting, hardwired into our boards at birth. Think about it: There is no experience you've had that you were not at the absolute center of.[9]

Everything else has to be communicated to us somehow, but our own experience of ourselves is real, alive, immediate, and central. Our perceptions of our experiences, of what we read and hear, of what we engage in the world are immediate and often seem automatically true. That does not mean they are fully true. That does not mean ours is the only valid experience or expression of reality in any given moment. Many of us come from communities that teach us not to be self-centered. However, Wallace reminds us that it is natural for us to see the world out of our own worldview and experiences. This is what we know. The danger comes when we don't recognize that we are doing this, when we use those experiences as the only valid way of experiencing the world, and/or when we develop lenses of fear or disregard toward other perspectives and ways of being in the world.

8. Wallace, *This is Water,* 33.
9. Ibid., 35–39.

One example of this might be the now internet famous case of a white woman who reportedly called the police on two African American men who were barbecuing.[10] We can take this case as an illustration of larger dynamics. When we are taught that the world is a scary place and when we are taught that some people (African Americans, men, maybe all people) are potentially dangerous, this shapes our lenses and we can feel that any situation is one of suspicion under the right circumstances. When we see or hear something that we do not recognize from our particular frames of seeing the world, we search to name it. Sometimes we get it wrong, especially if we are afraid.

My friend Arthur Kelly reflects on this phenomenon, "The human need to name is a way of resolving the unknown. I hear a sound in the middle of the night, and I must find a way to ease the fear it produces because the sound may be anything and will become anything until I am able to name it as the ice cube dispenser, the dripping faucet, the tree branch blowing in the wind, etc."[11] We create narratives to help us understand what we fear and why we fear it. Those narratives may only be partial. They also may be untrue.

These fears of the unknown show up in different ways. So do the narratives we tell ourselves and each other to explain them. They sometimes show up pointed at different people groups. They show up in our fear of losing our role or position in society, our fear of losing jobs in economic uncertainty, and/or our fear of losing loved ones to violence or illness or disaster. It is not uncommon to fear these things. But how do we answer our questions about the unknown? What narratives do we draw on and why do we draw on those narratives?

Another way that our fear of the unknown shows up is in "slippery slope" arguments. We fear that if *this step happens,* then *this other much larger thing* will inevitably happen. Slippery slopes are often debunked as logical fallacies because they are based on assumptions that a "relatively small first step will inevitably lead to a chain of related (negative) events,"[12] ignoring that the chain is not inevitable. Slippery slope arguments shut down conversations and the ability to thoughtfully discern whether or not the step in question has to lead to the larger conclusion we fear. They also reveal our fears sitting below the surface. We fear what might be at the

10. See the community's response in Holson, "Hundreds in Oakland Turn Out."
11. Kelly, email conversation, June 11, 2018.
12. Information is Beautiful, "Rhetological Fallacies."

bottom of that slope. We also fear because we simply do not know what might happen next.

Fear of Being Wrong

Often underneath our fear of the unknown the greater question is: What happens if we are wrong? Wallace's quote above reminds us that we are often wrong or at least not completely right. Many of us do not particularly like this. Some of us are downright afraid of it.

Sometimes we are afraid to be wrong because our identity is tied up in rightness. If we are wrong, what will that say about us? As a professor I can relate to that. The nature of my position sometimes comes with assumptions about what being "an expert" means. These messages can produce the fear of being wrong. A healthy dose can be helpful in keeping me diligent in my work. It is not helpful, however, when it becomes immobilizing.

Lately I have begun learning Spanish. I am a native English speaker. I simply do not already know how to think, decipher, and/or speak in the Spanish language. I also simply cannot learn if I don't risk making mistakes and demonstrating that I don't yet know everything. In Spanish as well as in my job, I do my work to continue to responsibly learn everything I can. I also do my work to humbly recognize where my own limitations are and resist that need to be an expert on everything. Discovering areas that I still need to learn does not make me a bad professor; it makes me a better one. It also makes me a more human one, one that students can connect with on a different level in our continued learning together.

Sometimes it feels like the stakes are higher, though. Sometimes we are afraid of being wrong because we are afraid that if we are wrong about fill in the blank, we may be wrong about so much more. We fear the larger worldview consequences and what that means for our lives and what we thought we knew about the world. For faith communities, sometimes we are afraid to be wrong because our understandings of our own salvation might be tied to rightness on particular issues. We are afraid of getting it wrong with eternal consequences.

Sometimes we don't want to be wrong not for our own sakes, but for others'. We recognize that ideas have implications for how we act and we don't want to cause harm. We are afraid of saying the wrong thing or doing the wrong thing or offending someone. We want to come alongside others. We want to show support. Sometimes we just don't know what to say or do or what not to say or what not to do. We don't want to get it wrong, so we freeze.

But truth and love sometimes require risk. The voices in chapters 2–5 will help us with this. Sometimes our fear helps by serving as an initial check, a filter keeping us from jumping in too soon and causing further harm. However, sometimes our fear can hinder us from jumping in at all. Sometimes it freezes our ability to speak or do and, therefore, inhibits our ability to learn and our opportunities to help. Sometimes we can let our fear close our mouths for a moment and open our ears. Sometimes, however, we have to risk opening our mouths and moving our feet anyway. Choosing to stumble forward with courage even in our fear can help us to learn in failures and successes. The voices in chapters 2–5 will help us with this as well.

Fear of Losing Security

Perhaps the fear that looms the largest in many of our communities in this moment is a fear of insecurity. In fact, as Scott Bader-Saye says in *Following Jesus in a Time of Fear*, it seems in our time, security has become "the new idol before whom all other gods must bow."[13]

Fear of insecurity leads us to treat others not as neighbors but "as potential threats."[14] When we fear the loss of security, protection and safety become our dominant virtues. Bader-Saye talks about this using the example of parenting practices today. When we parent out of fear, "we begin thinking primarily about what we want to prevent and avoid rather than what we want to encourage and develop."[15] We become hyper-vigilant about threats and less attentive to the formation of values and character. It is important to be thoughtful, to anticipate harm, and to work to keep our children (and ourselves) safe. Safety communicates love. However, it is problematic when the practices of keeping safe become the primary or exclusive value. Safe is not the whole of love. It is not the whole of wellness or shalom or the kin-dom of God.[16] Is there something more that we want

13. Bader-Saye, *Following Jesus*, 28.

14. Ibid., 31.

15. Ibid., 14.

16. I am using the word kin-dom to take cues from theologians who challenge the systems of hierarchy and dominance that the word "kingdom" sometimes indicates and to better articulate the communal reality of the image of the kingdom of God as described in Scripture.

to be known for beyond simply people who care about safety and protection? What are those things?

If protecting our security becomes our primary or exclusive value, then our posture leads us to clutch and to defend. Our posture toward others becomes suspicion. This posture makes welcome and hospitality difficult. It makes generosity difficult. It makes listening difficult. When we are afraid, it is harder to learn and understand. If security becomes our major virtue, protection from all potential harm takes our primary energy. "Only by becoming invulnerable can we find absolute security and invulnerability can be had only by fencing ourselves off from all danger or destroying everyone and everything that poses a possible threat to our well-being."[17] There are significant implications when living in a primary mode of protection and security regarding how we view "the other." Becoming invulnerable makes love impossible.

Fear Producing Fear

In acting out of our fears, we not only run the risk of making things unwelcoming for others, but we potentially contribute to making things unsafe for ourselves and others as well. When we are acting out of fear, we are not always acting out of good judgment.

My friend Sebastian gives an example of this in his life. Sebastian and his wife have cared for several children—both biological and foster, currently and in the past. This sometimes requires creative juggling on the part of the adults in the family to make sure everyone gets what they need. One day, in a moment of this juggling, Sebastian called a rideshare company to pick up his fifteen-year-old foster son who was living with them at the time to take him to early basketball practice before school. He recounts the experience of watching the driver's expression as he pulled up, the sky still dark in the early morning hours, and saw Sebastian (not a small man) and his son, a 6'+ African American teenager behind him. As they approached the car, the driver refused to roll down the window to talk to them. Then, as Sebastian's son went to get into the car, as Sebastian tells it, the driver, clearly afraid and frantic, yelled "get out, get out! I'm not taking this ride!" This response was more than an inconvenience for Sebastian and his family. It was a moment of creating potential danger. The driver's response made things potentially dangerous for the driver's next passengers while his body took

17. Bader-Saye, *Following Jesus*, 92.

its time to calm down physiologically and emotionally. It also made things potentially unsafe for Sebastian and his son. This driver, clearly afraid, now knows their address. Fear can produce reasons for others to fear.

There is evidence of this all throughout the following chapters. People from the immigrant, Muslim, LGBTQ+, and African American communities know that others are afraid of them, even if they don't always understand why. They see people respond out of this fear and it creates new fears within them. How do we love people who are afraid of us? How do we love those who we ourselves fear?

Is All Fear Bad?

We know that not all fear is bad. We sometimes need it. But fear can be scarring and the prolonged experience of it corrodes the body, mind, heart, and soul. Fear is designed to communicate to us when we are in danger. If we are constantly feeling in danger, we have significant questions to ask about our world, our place within it, and our perceptions of it.

The point is not to get rid of our intrinsic fear mechanism. The point is to exercise our thoughtful discernment regarding what actually poses a legitimate threat to us and what does not. The point is to address the messages telling us who to fear and how much to fear them and discern whether or not these messages are true.

Our fear often comes because we want to protect those we love. So what if our love also extends to strangers, neighbors, so-called enemies, and the world? As Bader-Saye asserts, "following Jesus will mean surrendering the power that masquerades as security in order to love the neighbor and welcome the stranger."[18] This is one thing this book is about, asking the question, "How can we maintain the posture of the open hand toward a world that scares us?"[19]

We do not have to do it alone. In fact, perhaps our feelings of loneliness and isolation are what often produce some of our fears of the other, our fears of doing or saying the wrong thing, and/or our fears of insecurity. We need not run away from our fears, but we may need to look them in the eyes and try to understand and name them. We need to explore where they came from. We need to understand how large the threat actually is and to what/whom. We also need to address the question of how legitimate those

18. Ibid., 22.
19. Ibid.

threats are and whether or not they need to stay legitimate. For communities of faith, we also need to ask: What does it look like to engage in a way that reflects the character of God in the world and that not only respects the human-ness of those different from ourselves but also moves us into a space where we can participate in and experience concrete love in those relationships? We need to think critically about whether or not our fears are compatible with a life of faith patterned after the way of Jesus and the bigger vision of the kin-dom of God in the world. Fear can become commodified, moralized, or weaponized. We don't have to let it, but we may have to make some adjustments.

My sister-in-law is a police officer. She is surrounded everyday by people who are not at their best and who are in the midst of choices that are not among their best. That might be what life is like for some of us. It may be difficult to form an alternative view of human-ness in these moments. Yet, that does not excuse us from it. In order to act a new world into being, we may need to recognize both the reality as it is as well as believe in our capacity to imagine and model a reality more like one we hope for.

In order to participate in creating a reality that is deeper and wider than what we are accustomed to, we need to get to know those deemed as "other." In doing so, we will have some decisions to make. In chapters 2–5, I will introduce you to some people I love. These neighbors identify with some of the communities feeling particular pressure and igniting particular fears. They are also feeling particular fears. In order for us to speak to our fears and increase in love we need these voices. In order to love our neighbors, strangers, and even so-called enemies, we need to hear from them. We cannot love what we don't yet know.

ALWAYS BACK TO LOVE

Love is Central

We started with fear, but in essence, love is what this whole book is about. I have chosen to model my life after the life and teachings of Jesus, a lower-economic, colonized, Middle Eastern Jewish man as told in biblical narratives and throughout Christian history. When I look to Jesus, everything centers on love. In fact, in the biblical text we find a story of someone coming up to Jesus and asking him: If we skinny the whole thing down, what is actually required of us? As the story goes, Jesus answers this bold question by pointing to his religious heritage and giving us what we often call the Great Commandments. We see them in the verses just a few pages ago: Love God with everything you are and everything you have and, in so doing, love your neighbor and/as yourself. Love is central. Everything else hinges upon love.

As Jesus followers it is then up to each of us to ask the question of what it means to be faithful, responsible lovers in our time and place. In the chapters to follow, our neighbors will help us to answer that question from their experiences. Here are also a couple of handles from my tradition to help us as we think about what our neighbors tell us.

Love is Practical

Think back to the example of my son's allergies. An act of providing food is often an act of love. However, if I offer him food that is toxic to his body, that is not love, that is harm, regardless of what my intention was. Learning what is toxic and what isn't to people is an act of love. Learning what connects as love and what does not is an act of love. Adjusting to these needs is not trouble; it is an act of welcome and love. It is also very simple and very practical. Love often is. And providing that kind of love requires a knowing.

Many of us grew up in communities where we heard or perhaps have even said, "God loves everybody, so we do, too." I wonder what kind of love this is. Can you love someone you don't know? We can have warm feelings or, at least not hard feelings, or perhaps the openness to the possibility of loving everyone out there in the universe. But I don't know how a distant universal love can be received as actual love. Can love be generic? Can love be abstract? I don't think so. That sounds like the idea of love, maybe the seeds of love. It doesn't sound like love itself. Love itself is much more concrete.

Love itself sounds more like gifts meeting needs. It sounds like being heard. It feels like warm food in a hungry belly. It looks like a friend beside you when it feels like the rest of the world is against you. It comes out of knowing a need and moving heaven and earth to meet it. Love is never detached; it is connected. It is not abstract; it is particular. It is personal. It is practical. It is specific. It is active. We will hear more about this in the chapters to come.

I come from a particular faith tradition that looks to two theologically and ethically loaded terms—holiness and unity—to make sense of how we live out that love in the world.[20] In my Wesleyan-Holiness tradition, taking its cues from the theology and practice of John Wesley, holiness is not primarily understood through the lens of separation. Rather, the marker of holiness is someone ever-growing in love. In other words, we do not become holy by protecting ourselves from all that we perceive isn't holy. We become holy and show that holiness in a life and a process that works to become a person who is so full of love that there simply isn't room for anything that isn't love. This leads us to cross boundaries that others might not cross. It leads us to develop relationships that others might not develop. It leads us to learn what life is like for the "other" so that we might love them better and be loved by them. It leads us to ask what looks, sounds, and feels like love to them, listen to their response, and weed out what doesn't.

Love is Both Personal and Structural

This kind of concrete and practical love is also structural, social, and systemic. Love is specific but it is not purely individualized. The process of learning what life is like for our neighbors takes into account how the structures we participate in and the circumstances or environments we find ourselves in have profound impact on us and how we live our lives.

On the structural level, love requires a stake in another's life. It means noticing which bellies regularly go hungry and asking why that is so. It means listening deeply to the one who is hungry and their assessment of the "why." It is following their lead so as to not simply offer a meal to a hungry person, day after day, but to interrupt the system that perpetuates hunger.

But we are getting a little bit ahead of ourselves.

The point, as we head into the rest of the book, is: We can agree that God calls us to love our neighbors. We can agree that this love is a central component to what it means to live a life following the way of Jesus as well as for many other faith traditions. But how do we love someone we have been taught to fear? How do we know what feels like love to our neighbors if we do not know them? Can love really be love if it doesn't result in a greater knowing and relationship between the lover and the beloved? These

---

20. I have explored further how I understand the way the Church of God (Anderson, IN), as a Wesleyan-Holiness church, has understood that love through holiness and unity in my chapter in Crawford, Dodrill, and Wilson, *Holy Imagination,* 161–74. Check that out there or dig into your own denomination's heritage.

are some of the most important questions that I almost never hear people ask. They are questions that ground this book.

FINALLY, STORY THREE

Recently, I participated in a workshop where my friends Juan Carlos La Puente and Ron Werner helped a group of people from a few local churches think through what it means to be long-term invested in the work of caring for their neighborhoods. In that workshop, Juan Carlos told a story about visiting his brother's family while his niece was very young. He recounted a moment while holding his niece on his lap when she began to play with his beard. At first her touch was gentle and curious. In her exploration, however, she soon began to tug harder and dig her fingertips into Juan Carlos's skin. It hurt. From across the room, Juan Carlos's sister-in-law noticed him wincing and pulling away and, as he tells it, she said to him clearly and directly, "Juan Carlos, you have to let her learn what it is to touch you gently."

Sometime later, while he was deep in prayer and contemplative practice, that experience came back to Juan Carlos's mind with a truth that rung out within and from his heart. That truth, he tells us, is, "You need to suffer the learning of the other. And others are suffering my learning. Others are cleaning up what I leave behind."[21]

Sometimes we may feel isolated but we are not alone. We are connected in ways that many of us simply may never understand. If the beating of a butterfly's wings can affect weather patterns across the world, one decision can affect other people's lives. We are not alone and our learning is not in isolation. Others are impacted by our uncertainties. Others are impacted by our fears. The good news is that we can relieve some of that suffering by deciding to learn. The people we hear from in this book may be some of those who are suffering our learning. We have both an opportunity and a responsibility to receive what they say in these pages. I do not promise this is easy work. It is not. But it is possible. It can even be joyful. And it is ours to do.

It is also not ours alone. Jesus was a boundary-crosser. He did not see those who were outside of dominant religious practices in his community as untouchable. He sought them out and saw them. He stopped for them. He allowed them to interrupt his life. He recognized that they were our teachers. He called and showed them that they were beloved by God.

21. La Puente and Werner, "Organizing for Social Change."

He demonstrated his holiness by being with those deemed unholy by the religious structures of his day. He reminded people that God, a God who hears the cries of the oppressed and the suffering, who is found in places where life is being lost, is the creator of all people. All people. You. Me. Your neighbors. And I'd like to introduce you to some of mine.

PART II

The Voices

#RACEAND: AN EXCURSUS ON INTERSECTIONS

THE AMAZING PEOPLE YOU will meet in the next four chapters are categorized according to one major component of their identity. However, it is important to note that we cannot reduce anyone to a singular identity component alone and no one group is uniform in how they experience the realities of that particular identity marker. All of us are made up of multiple identities—our race, gender, sexual orientation, class status, religion, dis/ability, education, etc. These pieces come together in complicated and sometimes contradictory ways.[1]

For example, my experience as a white, middle-class, straight woman in the US is different from a white, middle-class straight man in the US. It also differs from the experiences of an African American, middle-class straight woman; a Latinx,[2] middle-class, queer woman; a white, lower-class, straight woman, etc. Each of our identity markers can have an impact on how we experience the other components of our overall personhood. We cannot be reduced to any one component. Nor can we ignore any of the components.

1. Check out the series of #RaceAnd videos on YouTube to get a sense of how this works in people's lives.

2. Latinx is a term describing someone of Latin American descent. It is a gender-neutral alternative to the commonly heard Latino or Latina.

My point here is there are some shared realities. Other realities vary widely, even wildly. The people who were courageous enough to offer their stories here illustrate both of those. Sometimes it will seem like we can generalize. Even so, it is important to keep in mind that the intersectional experiences of our multiple identities create unique experiences and circumstances for each of us. They shape the ways we tell our stories. They shape the ways we read others' stories. Both the common experience of being human and the particular components of each of our human-ness are vital in getting to know someone. They are also both important elements in understanding our own fears and learning what feels like love to us and to another.

CHOOSING YOUR OWN ADVENTURE

So, now you have a choice to make, a "Choose Your Own Adventure" of sorts. This book is part of a bigger project that includes four short documentary video portraits, one to go with each of the chapters from chapter 2 to chapter 5. From here, you may:

- Simply dive in and continue reading.

- Go to www.loveinatimeoffear.com to watch the videos and get to know Victor, Sameya, Sarah, and Hakeem before reading about them and their communities.

- Have your phone or computer handy while you read and let Victor tell you his story while you read chapter 2, let Sameya tell you her story while you read chapter 3, let Sarah tell you her story while you read chapter 4, and let Hakeem tell you his story while you read chapter 5.

- Or, if you are reading this book as a part of a group, go to www.loveinatimeoffear.com where you will find a guide with some discussion questions for using this book and the videos with groups. This toolkit is designed with faith communities or neighborhood groups in mind to process what you are learning and thinking together.

Choice made? Breathe deep and let us begin.

2

I'm Trying to Live Until Tomorrow

Full-on Fear, Fake Love, and Being
an Immigrant in the US Today

I DON'T REMEMBER IF the day was sunny or cloudy. I don't remember if it was warm or cold, dry or wet. I don't remember what I was wearing, what we were talking about, or who was driving by. The only thing I remember is walking face first into a spider web.

Once you've walked face first into a spider, you can never be the same again.

At least I wasn't.

We can come up with plenty of reasons for why I didn't see it coming. Maybe it was cloudy and the sunlight wasn't hitting it just right. Maybe I was thinking about other things and simply didn't think to wonder if there was a spider web across my path. Maybe it was because I was trying to be attentive to my little one. But there I was, walking with my son, having just picked him up from preschool, headed to help him load up into the car to go home, when . . . (what's the right sound for a spider hitting a face?). It wasn't violent. It wasn't loud. But I was changed. You can't undo walking face first into a spider.

In the moment, my instincts took over and I sprang into action. Blood pressure spiking, I reached up to grab the spider with lightning speed and I threw that fat, unsuspecting spider to the ground in one quick motion, all unbeknownst to my son. Spider removed, I then took a moment to breathe, to let my adrenaline start to slow back down, and cleared what I could of the web off my face and hair as we walked to the car. And, in a move that Saint Francis of Assisi would be proud of, I whispered a fast apology to and prayer for the spider.

But I was not the same person any longer. Walking face first into that spider changed the way I walk in the world. Some moments are like that.

I had a face-first-into-a-spider-web moment in my classroom a few months later. Every spring I teach a class called Christian Social Concern. I have changed this class countless times. It is not perfect. Yet, I love it every time. I love the ways that my students and I learn together from each other and our neighbors and co-workers in our shared city. I look forward to it every year and keep an eye on my roster as students begin to register.

This particular year there was only one student on my roster who I did not already know: Gimena. So, when the first day of class came, I was watching for her. In she came with a posture that said she was coming in on the edges to check things out before making her decision about what kind of space and what kind of class this was going to be. She was clearly interviewing me. Her brilliant and wary eyes were full of fire. She entered the space with a quiet power. She was watching, maybe for signs that she could trust us, maybe for ways to survive the class for the next fifteen weeks. Maybe both.

I remember the moment when she decided it was worth the risk to find out if she could indeed trust us. She leaned in. Her eyes, still fierce and alive, were preparing to open up worlds for us. None of us has been quite the same since.

Gimena shared with us the fears that she has lived with her whole life being a part of a mixed citizenship status family. She shared with us her fear of being left alone to care for her younger siblings. She told of the trauma during a border crossing to return home, being held at one point away from her parents, and the sustained fear of being separated again. She told us of the pressure to get to twenty-one years old so that she could try to begin the process of sponsoring her family members. She told us of the pressure she carried to graduate with the kind of honors and networks that could help her land a good enough job to help her family buy a house, something currently impossible given that they cannot take out a bank loan. She shared with us her mother's determination that they would not accept any social service assistance, even though the need has been great at times, because she does not want to put their eligibility for residency at risk if that becomes a stipulation. The present fear in Gimena's eyes as she told us of her life seared me. The pressure she has carried for most of her life was, for many in the room, barely imaginable. For others it was far too familiar.

Gimena has papers. She is still afraid. Because for nearly her whole life, in the place she calls home, she has felt in her bones that her family is not wanted. She has also known that they need to be here. A life like this develops a type of resolve and determination and power in the people who live it. I see this nearly every day. It feels like a miracle. But it does not create feelings of being loved.

In one of her poems, Muriel Rukeyser asks the question-statement: "What would happen if one woman told the truth of her life" and answering her own question, she states, "The world would split open."[1] Gimena had the courage to speak the truth of parts of her life into a space where it was heard and the world was no longer the same. I saw proof in her classmates' faces. The "topics" we were studying had concretized, crystallized, cauterized. I saw proof on a reading analysis turned in at the end of class that day where a classmate had crossed out a statement he had made before class and wrote in the margin, "Not anymore. Not after today." We had had our spider in the face moment. The ways we walk in the world were changed.

Gimena's story is Gimena's story. It is unique to her and her family. It is also emblematic of the stories of countless other families. It is not isolated and it did not come out of nowhere. Gimena's story is part of a much larger history and current reality of immigration in the US.

THE FRAME

Immigration is a huge component to the story of the United States as a country. It has brought both opportunity and struggle to the people living here. Some of our ancestors came for opportunity. Some were displaced by others. Some have come because of necessity. Some were forced to be here. And here we are. Together. But not together. Figuring out how that operates and what that means continues to loom large in our narrative of US history and identity.

---

1. Rukeyser, "Käthe Kollwitz." You can read the poem in its entirety here: https://www.poetryfoundation.org/poems/90874/kathe-kollwitz.

As I write this, it has been forty days since President Trump signed an executive order amidst significant political pressure to stop the practice of separating families at the border. Those of us paying attention have seen images of children taken from their parents. We have heard their cries. And people all over the country, regardless of political orientation, have demonstrated outrage. We see evidence of this on social media, news stations, and on city streets. We see it in one couple's Facebook fundraiser whose goal to "raise $1,500 to help an immigrant family post bond" has now raised more than $17 million and counting.[2] The border, it seems, is not the only line that has been crossed.

Not long ago the US government briefly "shut down." This was not the first threatened or actual shut-down in recent months and one of the major impasses continues to be immigration. On the table are whether to pass the continuation of DACA or a Dream Act, how to attend to border security, addressing sanctuary cities and their rights, and what to do about the rest of the eleven million undocumented people in the country who are not "Dreamers" and who are also not violent criminals. When it comes to the "immigration debate," it is clear that things are still heating up. Partisan divides are deep. Families are living in constant fear.

On this topic, the sometimes competing values of the US are on full display. Most people are concerned about both the humanity of our immigrant neighbors and the need for thoughtful border policies in an insecure world. The differences are often in which direction we lean more heavily and, even more often, how we are characterized by those on the "other side."

On one end are those declaring that the US needs to be a place where others, especially those fleeing violence, can find new life and opportunity. These voices often draw on beliefs that God is a God of all people, the US is a land of opportunity and freedom, and hold, therefore, that it is our moral obligation to welcome these neighbors. Welcome is emphasized.

On the other end are those who declare that immigrants and refugees are welcome but only if they have come lawfully or are from certain parts of the world, given a variety of factors. These voices often draw on beliefs that the law is the moral code and the pathway to follow and that weak borders represent a security threat to us and our families. Law is emphasized.

Passionate debates can bring out our best and our worst. In our best moments, we work together to understand one another and hold the important pieces together, following the lead of those most directly impacted.

2. All Things Considered, "Millions Raised for Immigrants."

In our worst moments we dehumanize one another, as evidence in the comment, "Send those things back," posted on Facebook in response to a group of Christian ministers gathering to stand up for DACA[3] recipients and immigrant rights.

Regardless of how we feel about borders, immigrants are not things. They are flesh, blood, and bone. They are heart, soul, and mind. They are people created in the image of God, beloved by God, and seen by a God who, by the testimony of the Christian scriptures, hears the cries of the foreigner and calls us to figure out what it means to do likewise.

In most of our family histories is a story of something that propelled our ancestors (or us) to find a place in this land, be it fleeing from trauma, seeking new opportunities for the future, or a combination of the two. And in most of our family histories, there are parts of that story that were met with welcome and care—people making room for us in their lives and in their spaces; parts that were met with hardship, suspicion, and discrimination—people afraid of who we were or what we might bring; and parts that caused harm to others, particularly to families that are native to this land, who have carried the burden for generations, and who we rarely stop to think about or thank for making room for us.[4] Responsibility is wide when we allow ourselves to dig deep. So is the divide on what to do.

There is no shortage of messages about immigrants. These messages are political. They are also theological. We see this in Attorney General Jeff Sessions' use of Romans 13 as a means of justifying the separation of families and detaining of children. We see it in his own denomination as they filed charges against these statements as violation of church discipline.

---

3. The Consideration of Deferred Action for Childhood Arrivals (DACA) is a program that started in 2012 wherein "the Secretary of Homeland Security announced that certain people who came to the United States as children and meet several guidelines may request consideration of deferred action for a period of two years, subject to renewal. They are also eligible for work authorization. Deferred action is a use of prosecutorial discretion to defer removal action against an individual for a certain period of time. Deferred action does not provide lawful status." Read more at the US Citizenship and Immigration Services website at https://www.uscis.gov/archive/consideration-deferred-action-childhood-arrivals-daca. In essence, DACA provides undocumented immigrants who were brought to the US as children a stay on deportation and a permit to work lawfully. It is a two year certification that is subject to renewal. It is also currently under question all together.

4. To learn more from and about our Native American neighbors and hosts, see the new documentary "A Home Divided," by filmmaker Sebastian Rogers about Native American activist Mark Charles.

theological convictions, and social teachings.[5] We see it in the response of the Reclaiming Jesus movement, and similar local movements all over the country, to oppose messages like Sessions's and work for the integrity of the Christian faith by reminding us of the later verses of Romans 13 as well, beginning with verse 8: "Owe no one anything, except to love one another; for the one who loves another has fulfilled the law."[6] Are love and law in conflict here? For many it feels like the soul of the nation is at stake.

Christianity, too, is a story of migration. In the first chapters of the biblical text, Adam and Eve are sent from the garden where they were created (Gen 3). Abraham was called away from his homeland into another (Gen 11–12). Joseph's, Daniel's, and Ruth's stories center on their realities away from their homelands (Gen 37–50, Daniel, Ruth). The histories and prophets tell stories of exile and return to and from lands far away (Nehemiah, Jeremiah, Ezekiel, etc.). Jesus's family fled as refugees during Herod's reign (Matt 2). These are to name only a few.

Therefore, perhaps it is no surprise that Christian scriptures are full of calls to care for strangers/foreigners. The call to care for the foreigners in our midst is connected with the memory of our ancestors being strangers in a foreign land wherein God heard their cries and delivered them (Lev 19:33, Deut 10). The message is not mixed. It is clear. God delivered them from those who would not welcome them. God delivered them from those who exploited and benefitted from their labor. God delivered them from those who did not see them as God's image-bearers. God heard their cries and delivered them. It was not good news to Pharaoh. It was very good news for these children of God who were strangers in a land not their own.

And yet, the theological responsibility to thoughtfully engage this "issue" has been underplayed in some circles that formerly advocated for it. A recent article reported that the group now "least likely" to believe that the US has "a responsibility to accept" immigrants and refugees is white Evangelical Christians. This has not always been the case. It is also not true for all Evangelical Christians, but it does represent a shift in recent years for some groups of people within the Christian community to no longer see welcoming immigrants and refugees as something that has to do with living Christ-like lives. "This is not a Biblical issue," stated the first comment listed after the Christian Broadcasting Network (a network known to be conservative) posted an article referring to several biblical passages

---

5. Burke, "Jeff Session's Church Just Charged Him."

6. See this statement and other resources at http://www.reclaimingjesus.org.

reminding Christian faith communities to "Treat refugees the way you want to be treated," (drawing on Lev 19), and "Invite the stranger in,"[7] (referring to Matt 25). Calls and commands to care for the stranger run thick throughout Christian scriptures.[8] So why the shift to consider it political and not biblical?

The immigration debate has become one between "liberals" and "conservatives." In many instances, it has become more partisan than theologically connecting. It has not always been so, just as our borders have not always been where they are and our policies around them have varied over our history.[9] We do not have to draw sides according to such sharp party lines. The outrage over family separation in the summer of 2018 has demonstrated this. In fact, as people of faith, we must give very careful thought to where we land in terms of how the party lines are drawn regarding immigration. We need to give careful thought regarding whether we have given over the voice of morality to either party.

And it is clear that fear as well as calls to love are alive here. So, what are we honestly afraid of when thinking about the dynamics of immigration? What does it mean to take seriously the call to love and dignity in the midst of something with such high stakes for so many?

False Assumptions and the Fears Behind Them

Sometimes we reveal our fears in the messages and assumptions we listen to or believe. When it comes to immigrants, assumptions are many. Christian ethicist Miguel De La Torre articulates and debunks six common assumptions stated about undocumented people to help us decipher fact from fiction. In this list of assumptions, fear is a present companion.

To the assumption that, "They are using up our services and contributing nothing financially," De La Torre points out that undocumented immigrants contribute $10 billion to the US economy without being able to benefit from Social Security. They pay in. They cannot draw out. Therefore, "Ironically," says De La Torre, "the undocumented are supporting Social

---

7. Bump, "The Group Least Likely."

8. See a list compiled by the United Church of Christ here: http://www.ucc.org/justice_immigration_worship_biblical-references-to.

9. See De La Torre, *Trails of Hope and Terror.*

Security and Medicare for the next generation of documented Americans" while being unable to draw benefits themselves.[10]

To the assumption that, "They are taking away our jobs," De La Torre points out the coinciding of immigration waves with low unemployment rates and economic growth. He also points out that much "undocumented immigrant labor tends to be low skilled when compared to native workers and seldom threatens native-born workers' jobs."[11] A common response is that immigrants are doing jobs that nobody else wants (even though many immigrants come with significant education and credentials). There is truth here. However, we cannot rest with that response nor with the response above regarding social services. As people concerned to love our neighbors, we need to ask significant questions regarding the need for our economy to have a low-paid, "disposable" workforce and whether our systems of service are just.

And I wonder if behind these assumptions about job and social services stealing lurks the fear of not being able to provide or care for ourselves or our families, a fear that everything we have worked for will not be available to us when we need it. It seems that both these first two are undergirded by a fear of economic security. True, we live in economically insecure times. We could ask some difficult questions of the economy and who is benefiting and who is suffering in it. We could engage in analysis regarding how quickly some job sectors have changed. The problem comes when our real fear of not being able to care for those we love leads us to blame others who are also economically vulnerable in jobs that many of us may not even consider.

To the assumption that, "They increase the rate of crime," De La Torre points out the low percentage rate of noncitizens in US prisons (federal and state), aside from immigrant-specific detention centers.[12] Our fear seems to be that this will change any moment. Given the rise in violence worldwide, the increase in mass shootings, and the threats we hear on a regular basis, I can see why we fear more violence. Violence is prevalent. We need to continue to analyze the ways that our values and our divisions perpetuate violence. However, harm occurs when we map our real fear of the growing threat of violence onto whole groups of people, many of whom have lived peacefully and constructively within our neighborhoods for years. It is, in

10. De La Torre, "For Immigrants," 78.

11. Ibid.

12. Ibid., 79.

fact, often our immigrant neighbors who are more likely to be the recipients of violence than perpetrators due to the implicit bias that many carry toward immigrants.[13]

This assumption is often added to the assumption that, "They are lawbreakers who enter the country illegally." Both of these might point to another sense of insecurity we hold, one of physical safety. This assumption also fails to recognize the circumstances and processes that bring immigrants to our country to begin with. To this, De La Torre reminds us that we often harmfully group people into categories that simply do not fit. "[A]ccording to the Department of Homeland Security, about 75 percent of today's immigrants have permanent visas. Of the 25 percent who are undocumented, 40 percent overstayed their temporary visas."[14] Many immigrants followed the paths available to them to come here. Others have found that to do so by legal channels, with people waiting for more than twenty years for family-sponsored visas[15] and given the prohibitive costs of the applications and lawyer fees, the lines are simply longer than they can safely wait. When the threat is now, twenty years is too long to wait. When the threat is now, you have to move.

As thoughtful people we need to also be aware of how "Stereotyping aliens as lawbreakers, and by extension all Hispanics as lawbreakers, appeals to racism for political gains."[16] "Immigrants" is not a uniform category, although a certain image of "the immigrant" has lately been constructed in our national consciousness. There seems to be a fear of loss underneath this, perhaps a fear of being "taken over." This, too, connects with insecurity. There are also potentially racist undertones with significant implications for our actions. A fear of "the other" runs the risk of demonizing rather than welcoming potential neighbors.

Finally, to the assumption that, "They are bringing diseases into the country," De La Torre points out that the Centers for Disease Control (CDC) "does not believe that the incidence of diseases attributed to the undocumented immigrants is important enough to cover or report."[17] Fear of

13. A majority of Americans demonstrate an implicit bias and association of "goodness" with people with lighter skin than with darker skin. This is not conscious association but a subconscious bias that often we have absorbed in growing up. You can explore implicit bias more with the link in the Appendix.

14. De La Torre, "For Immigrants," 79.

15. Khimm, "How Long is the Immigration 'Line'?"

16. De La Torre, "For Immigrants," 79.

17. Ibid., 80. See more at www.cdc.gov.

immigrants as carriers of disease is a long-held fear and often not without cause as we know that migrants all over the globe have brought both richness in ideas and cultural practices as well as pathogens from other parts of the world. However, in this case, the fear has not been substantiated. This could be another example of subconscious biases against the "other" that in our history has sometimes been imagined as "dirty."[18] We might be able to infer this in President Trump's regrettable choice of words regarding the nations from which the US often receives immigrants.[19] The larger fear that lurks below this one might be our fear of our own mortality, our desire to protect ourselves from some unknown enemy. There is much to explore here.

It is perhaps ironic, as De La Torre points out, that the two phrases that appear most often in the Bible are "do not be afraid" and to take care of the "alien within your midst."[20] In our world, those two are not separate. To be able to genuinely and concretely care for the stranger in our midst we may need to actively work against our inherited fears and the false messages we receive. We need to ask difficult questions of what we hear in the messages surrounding us and the assumptions we carry. Following the first century refugee named Jesus asks no less.

As Fr. James Martin, SJ, stated in response to the President's comment referred to above:

> Why are we having all these people from sh#*hole countries come here?
>
> 1.) They are our brothers and sisters in need.
>
> 2.) They are often fleeing war, violence, or famine.
>
> 3.) There are children among them.
>
> 4.) The Old Testament asks us to care for the "alien."
>
> 5.) Jesus asks us to welcome the "stranger."
>
> 6.) Jesus asks us to love one another.
>
> 7.) We will be judged on how we care for the stranger.
>
> 8.) They come bringing hope.
>
> 9.) It's the right thing to do.

18. I chronicle this in my book, *Theology in the Age of Global HIV & AIDS*, especially in Part II.

19. Davis, Stolberg, and Kaplan, "Trump Alarms Lawmakers."

20. De La Torre, "For Immigrants," 80.

10.) That's who we are.

One more reason: Jesus himself was from a "sh#*hole" place. Nazareth was a minuscule town of 200 to 400 people, where people lived in small stone houses, and, say archaeologists, garbage (that is, s#*t) was dumped in the alleyways. "Can anything good come from Nazareth?" says Nathanael when he hears where the Messiah is from.

God, in other words, came from a "sh#*hole" place. And he pointedly asked us to welcome him whenever he appeared as a "stranger," or as one of our "least" brothers and sisters. That's why we have all these people come. Because Jesus came.[21]

Immigrants are not things. Their homelands are not "sh#*holes." They are people, often survivors of great trauma, who love their homelands and have made difficult choices that some of us simply cannot fathom. Immigrants are image bearers of God, beloved by God, and seen by a God who, by the biblical testimony, hears the cries of the foreigner and calls us to do likewise.

For many of us, as soon as we begin hearing comments like those above, we recognize how inflammatory they have been. If we are prone to be conflict avoidant, we might feel ourselves shrinking from the conversation altogether. Yet, for those of us who work to follow the ways of Jesus, welcoming the stranger and loving our neighbors is foundational. It is bedrock. We cannot shrink from the concerns that are deeply impacting our neighbors in need. So what does love look, sound, feel like for our neighbors impacted by the vagaries of immigration and the fears that go with it? And what doesn't look, sound, or feel like love right now?

THE CONVERSATIONS

Immigrants are not a uniform group, yet the classic picture of who an immigrant is in our time and place has been dominantly marked by certain characteristics in our minds, often someone from Latin American descent. Therefore, over the past several uncertain months, I sat down with a group of mixed documentation status Latinx students who are some of the brightest and strongest people on the planet and I put the questions about love to them. I heard stories of power and resilience, stories of trauma and fear,

---

21. Martin, "Why Are We Having all These People."

stories of uncertainties and necessary "life hacks," and I heard stories of help that was helpful and "help" that went wrong.

Erendira Villagomez (a radiant college student who overflows with go-getter energy, assertiveness, and not just a little rascaliness, even though she often carries the burden of the whole world) jumps in immediately with some concrete stories of love and not love. She shares a story of a friend who is a DACA recipient and who had to drop out of college this year due to the uncertainties around what will be next for him. Erendira laments that she wishes she could get him the money to finish at least his Associate Degree "so he wouldn't leave with useless credits. That would be love," she says. "And I know that's a very materialistic view but I know what that would mean to him because I know what that would mean to me."

Erendira continues, recognizing that for something to land as love, it comes not only out of sentimentality or convenience but a relationship proven in being willing to be interrupted for the sake of the other. "We'll put everything on pause to help each other in those ways."

The room agrees with head nods and knowing looks. Andy Rivas-Vazquez and Montse Astorga Ramos chime in with similar, concrete and practical examples. Andy (a confident, fiercely loyal, and deeply family oriented student leader who embodies sacrificial giving) talks about his girlfriend, who is a US citizen of native Hawaiian descent, and her offer to be listed as temporary guardian for Andy's younger siblings, who are also US citizens, if he and his parents were to be deported. This is not lip service but concrete action and action that carries risk.

"It brings me hope that there are people out there who are not in our situation but who still care deeply about us and will put themselves in the line of fire," Andy says.

Montse (one of the unassuming mama bears of the group, highly awarded for her brilliance in the classroom and in the field of social work and whose every cell overflows with joy, compassion, and life-giving power) offers two other examples from her own life of moments of concrete love. She talks about a classmate, Sandra Ramirez, who has her citizenship and who was coming to college from the same neighborhood as Montse. She mentions that Sandra gave her a ride to school every day for two years because Montse could not get her driver's license.

"She got up a little bit earlier every day to help without asking. She saw this need and she addressed it without ever asking or doubting or pushing to ask why I couldn't drive, you know? She just saw this need and stepped in and to me that was love. And it is way more tangible than anything else. It may seem very simple but it means so much."

The impact of that action meant that Montse did not have to think about how she was going to get to and from school every day. That was one thing removed from her very full plate of questions and pressures. That one thing made a big difference.

Montse goes on to give another example right after the 2016 Presidential election. Many immigrant families experienced significant fear and uncertainty in those moments directly after the results were announced (and in the months since) due to the way that President Trump talks about immigrants. Montse tells a story about how directly after the election, a mentor, Grace Kim, called her and offered an extra room in her house if Montse's family needed it.

"We never had to use it but just knowing that I had that was reassuring," Montse remembered. "I have family and friends who have given me money to pay for school because they know I don't have financial aid from the government. I hate feeling that because part of me wants to be independent but because of my situation I have to depend on that kind of love, which may seem materialistic, but that's really the need I have."

That is the second time the word "materialistic" is used. There seems to be a struggle in the conversation, a sense of not quite shame but borderline embarrassment or remorse in knowing that what most feels like love to them is really practical. Part of that is a result of coming from proudly hard-working families. I wonder if it is also an indictment on how we have perceived love culturally and theologically in the US. As we framed it in chapter 1, love is incredibly practical. It is concretely meeting people at their point of need and proving with action and presence that we want life for those we love in the points where their lives are being squeezed. I do not think that is always how love is portrayed in our churches or in our country. That seems to be affecting these students with an extra layer of unnecessary embarrassment.

Andy jumps in here again, "Sometimes the actions don't have to be big. Sometimes they're knowing there's a place or a friend who says they're there because sometimes we don't want to think about everything, we just want to get our heads away and be with a friend." Referring to Montse's comment about materialistic need, he adds, "it makes us feel like we're more human and on an equal playing field when we have access to those resources. Sometimes I have to work fifty times as hard just to get where you're at, so when people give you those tangible gifts, it makes you feel like a lot more human and like you're doing okay."

In that sense, Andy indicates, offering practical resources feels like love not simply because it meets that particular practical need, but it also relieves a layer of anxiety and pressure that goes with constantly needing to problem-solve the "how" of meeting those needs. It creates a much needed pressure valve.

Not all attempts and responses from others have felt like love, however, even from people who seem to be well-meaning. Erendira jumps back in here stating that what does not feel like love is when people say they love and care about you but then "vote against you."

"Literally," she says, "it's like the song by Drake, 'Fake Love.'" Everyone laughs. Then the tone turns serious. Erendira continues, "that is what I think of when you have those people who say they want to understand, say that they do understand and that they're there for me and they love me and always check in with me but at the end of the day, it's very surface."

Montse tells a story expressing a similar experience. "I think one of the biggest 'it looks like love but it isn't love' moments that happened to me was after the election happened. I posted something on Facebook and one of the leaders of the church I used to go to commented back, 'Trump is president but he is not God so don't be afraid.' Simultaneously he posted on his page about how he supported Trump and in his comment on my post he said, 'I love your family.' To me that was like a slap in the face. So, for me you need to realize that yes, you may have one friend who is undocumented but there's a whole group of people impacted. Yes, you might take care of your friend, but at the end of the day, many other people are also impacted. People don't have to be in your proximity or friends or family for you to care. I have a lot of people in my life who just care for me and my family and for me that's not enough. I wish they cared bigger."

The bigger understanding is what translates to different social action with an eye toward its impact on people in the whole immigrant community. It is beginning to realize how our lives are tangled up with one another and we do not have to believe in either/or and for/against, but to begin to creatively think about how our behaviors and our lives are connected to others.

Andy jumps in here. "I think people don't realize that their actions have consequences. Everybody is entitled to their own belief systems. If you want to believe I'm not supposed to be here, I'm not going to be in favor of your thinking but I'll still show love to you. Just know that decisions have impact on others. If you're seeking an economic boost or your own benefit or whatever, know that the other decisions that follow with it also impact everyone else. It comes at a cost. Even if people saw the election as a 'lesser of two evils,' what are the insights into which 'evil' you chose?"

Andy is offering a call to own the decisions we make, what we do agree with about any particular party or candidate or policy, what we do not agree with, and strongly consider who is negatively impacted by the consequences of those decisions. I think of Dietrich Bonhoeffer in situations like this. Bonhoeffer was a German theologian in WWII era Germany who was both committed to nonviolence and to protecting the communities being targeted by the Nazi regime. As such, Bonhoeffer had some difficult decisions to make. In his writings on ethics he articulates that sometimes the choice is not between a clear right and a clear wrong but varying levels of right and wrong mixed together. In those moments, what we have to think about is not how are we going to walk away clean and unscathed by this moment, but the questions are: Who are the people being crushed under the wheel of current practices/policies? How is the coming generation to have a chance to live?[22] Simply not having a preferable choice is not good enough.

To Andy, owning the impacts of our choices and not pretending that we are somehow exempt communicates more care than hiding or staying silent or justifying our rightness in the face of those deeply impacted in harmful ways. This is a step toward love in the form of respect and in the form of recognizing our own complicity or entanglement in things that are complicated. It might even include recognizing that we have privilege in this country if we are not directly impacted by these policies or stories.

Blanca Gaytan Farfan (a calm, quiet, and deeply respected power who, when she chooses to speak, speaks with a measured and deep wisdom of one who is constantly breaking ceilings and charting new paths) chimes in with another example of something that was intended as love but did not feel like it. "If people want to find ways to help they should do something about it. The question to us is often, 'What can I be doing? I feel so bad.' People should take their own active approach to do something."

In other words, we should do our own homework. We should take initiative.

---

22. To learn more about Bonhoeffer, see the film by Doblmeier, *Bonhoeffer: Pastor, Pacifist, Nazi Resister*.

Blanca continues, "If you really care about an issue, you're not going to be asking people who are directly affected, 'what can I do?'" Especially in high pressure moments. "It puts an additional layer of pressure on the person being targeted."

Montse jumps in with an example that impacted Veronica Jeronimo Martinez and Nelly Manzo Hernandez, two other Latinx students in the room who are US citizens. Montse starts, "It was really frustrating because, although they were the ones being harmed, the question was put to them, what should the person who harmed them do to make things right with them?" She continues, "Well, why wasn't the person who harmed them thinking about the depth of the harm and how he could make this better? It's kind of this paradox where 'yeah, we want your help,' but telling your story over and over is so exhausting that sometimes you just want to shut down."

Okay. There is a tricky intersection here. Let's say I am the teacher or minister or neighbor who is trying to navigate this situation. It is important to still center control and voice in the person who was harmed and re-empower them by making sure they get to decide what happens next. It is important to also be mindful to not ask them to do someone else's work for them. Those could sound like two different but related realities where in one, the perpetrator of harm needs to do their own work and then come to the table with listening ears and some solutions to offer for their own continued growth. In this example, the one who caused harm is listening to the voice of the one harmed but is not relying on the one harmed to be their exclusive teacher. If the one harmed has to carry the burden of also being the primary or exclusive teacher to the perpetrator of harm that brings the risk of re-traumatizing by putting more pressure on the one who has experienced trauma. Yet, it is still important for the one who has experienced harm to have the opportunity to exercise their power and voice and sense of control over what happens next. It is also important that actual learning happens for the one who caused harm. The balance sometimes sounds tricky. The key is deep listening.

"Asking someone what to do and asking their opinion are two different things," said Veronica (with her typical directness that demonstrates her power and vivacious energy, ready to tackle the world while also always ready to shift into bubbling laughter). "I was born here so I've always had an advantage but I have always been portrayed as someone who doesn't have advantage," she says as she lists some examples of this happening in her life.

In cases like this, "there's a difference between asking people 'what do you think' and 'what should I do.'"

Montse chimes in, responding to Veronica's comments, "it's a difference between placing the responsibility on the harmed as opposed to taking ownership or responsibility and then acting on it based on asking the person who was harmed what they think."

I ask the group for any examples of this happening in a loving and empowering way as this is a common scenario for many of them. They struggle to think of any.

"I don't have a positive experience with that," says Blanca. She begins to recount a situation where a member of the administration at her school, showing concern, approached her after a particularly charged political moment and asked, "what should I tell the board? What can I do to make this better for you and students like you?" At face value, this is a caring question. It came out of a sense of being motivated to show love and concern. And yet, remembers Blanca, "I think at that moment I was like, 'I have no idea.' I was still trying to process my experiences and the impact [the political decision] was going to have." She continues, "I understand the good intentions behind wanting to take some action and with a sense of urgency. But also, I don't know, it's hard to be in the position of being asked that when I have no idea."

We talk for a little while as a group about the difference between knowing and listening deeply to someone's story and listening for places where you can work and take action on their behalf rather than them telling you what you should do (and, therefore, having them work on your behalf), yet still taking cues from those most deeply impacted. Already having a knowing relationship is key. We talk about the importance of working to take cues from immigrant-led organizations who are mobilizing action steps to make concrete urgent differences in those moments and not putting all of the pressure on particular neighbors or friends.

Sometimes the individuals in our lives are not ready to mobilize a whole community but need a moment to breathe and think and take care of themselves in the midst of life-squeezing realities. Giving them that space is love. Treating them like others who you love who are having a hard time feels like love. In other words, bring them their favorite meal. Watch their kids. Spend time together. Run errands for them. Do what you would do in a relationship.

And often, the organizations growing out of immigrant communities and working on their behalf will rather rapidly put some toolkits and processes or events in motion for the other kind of broader work. What I hear from this particular group of young people as well as from immigrant-led organizations is to do the work of learning who those organizations are and be prepared to take your cues from them to support your immigrant friends and neighbors. This also is love. It shows that your concern goes beyond their particular intersection with your life but includes those who are in their other or wider communities. It also means that you are invested in the longer term work, with a different pace, out of genuine care and not only knee jerk responses in isolated moment. This is some of the bigger love Montse was talking about. You can circle back to your particular immigrant friends and loved ones for confirmation to see if what is suggested by the organizations feels helpful to them.

Andy jumps in to reinforce Blanca's thoughts, "I think people think that just because we're living this life, I don't know. People think we're some experts and have the solution when we're the ones impacted the most."

And sometimes "just surviving," Montse interjects.

Andy continues, "and we're not thinking about solutions. We could say, 'man, I wish I had papers.' Done deal. But like, that's about as far as we go. This is one of those situations that there isn't just one solution that you can just go to. Getting asked the question of 'what do you want me to tell them,' I don't even know what to tell myself."

Love in these situations may require patience and persistence on the side of the one who wants to help—two virtues that immigrants know far too well. These are also two virtues that helping communities, thirsty for quick fixes, sometimes fail at.

Montse adds, "I think it's so strange when that's the reality of political actions. They're so big but the implications impact everyday life and when you're in survival mode trying to figure out how to live, it's hard to come up with a solution to the big issues. I don't know, I'm trying to live until tomorrow. I can't think that far ahead."

Montse, Andy, and Blanca all begin to recount talking to a particular mutual friend, telling her their stories separately. Remembering her response, Andy recounts, "It was like a wake-up call. It's just like I said, sometimes people don't understand the consequences that these things will have for someone else's life. It's like she was realizing, 'oh, so these are the consequences that came with this one simple decision.' She said that she stayed up all night crying because she couldn't believe that what she had done had those consequences."

Sometimes you just don't know until you know and until you have a reason to know. Recognizing that we haven't had a reason to know demonstrates our privilege. Others are suffering our learning. The love of neighbor asks us to challenge that.

In early 2018, the BBC put out a video called "The Missing—Consequences of Trump's Immigration Crackdown."[23] This video traces the impacts of recent immigration policy on a rural community in Washington, a community that largely voted Republican in the 2016 election and had thought that Trump's immigration platform sounded like what the country needs. They did not realize the impact of that platform on their own community, their own neighbors, the people who they went to church with, who went to school with their kids.

Flint Wright, Long Beach, WA, police officer and Trump voter articulated in this video the emotional "turmoil" that the community was facing when people they have known for years all of a sudden "are just gone," including twenty-five students from the local schools. Wright states, "Shame on me, but I didn't think about how it would actually play out with these people that I know." He continues:

> You cannot tell me that our community is better off or that the United States is better off because Mario has been shipped back to Mexico . . . It's easy to hear soundbites and say, yes, that's great policy. It's different when you're implementing it and you start seeing wait a minute this is actually affecting these peoples' lives and that . . . I didn't sign up for this. And shame on me for being shortsighted about it, okay? I mean fine, but it's not just. It's not just. To me.[24]

This illustrates exactly what Andy, Blanca, and Montse are talking about. Whenever we establish large scale policy, many more people will be impacted than we realize. To love is to think it through with our neighbors in mind and that takes actually knowing what life is like for them and realizing that it might be very different from our own in ways that we might not expect. It takes listening deeply and following their cues.

Erendira hits at the notion of privilege when she comments that she wishes people would ask themselves why our immigrant neighbors would

23. BBC, "The Missing."
24. Ibid.

come to the US. "For some of us, it wasn't a choice. I want to tell people to picture yourself as my dad at the age of twenty and my mom at nineteen. They have this child and they know bad people are going to come into town and take over part of their ranch. And they know in that moment that it's a life or death situation. I want you to decide what you're going to do. Are you going to choose to live and run away or are you going to choose to stay there? That's something that I wish people would understand because if they thought about their children and how much they love them and what they will do for their children, that's what my parents did. They love me so much that they would sacrifice anything. I know that other people who want to understand, if they think about their children and how much they would do for them, even if the government doesn't agree with what they're doing, you know?" She continues, "most people will do whatever you can to help your family survive. You just want to put yourself in a better spot. That's exactly what we're doing."

Silent head nods occur all over the room. Erendira continues, "I would want people to picture what it looks like to cross the border. The dangers, the expense, the process, that's how bad it is that our parents were willing to go through that and put us through that. The amount of people who died, assault, trauma, rape, a lot of people being scammed. If people knew those facts, they would understand what we're going through."

Tangible sacrifices were made and real trauma has been incurred. It is also ongoing.

Montse picks up with the theme of ongoing trauma. "Living with the sense of fear of deportation is traumatizing. Even just walking down the street, you have to think about things that people wouldn't. And crossing the border has impacted you and there's all this built up trauma that you have. You're dealing with past trauma plus continued trauma."

That is true for those who were brought across the border through no decision of their own. It is also true for parents who made that courageous risky decision on behalf of their families, not knowing what would be the result but knowing that they simply could not stay in their situation. It is also true for many Latinx people who were born here but have mixed-documentation status families. It is even true for many Latinx people who are full citizens but absorb the trauma due to assumptions and generalizations that are also leveraged against them with undertones of racism.

Erendira illustrates this trauma in her own life, "I remember going to school scared as heck because I'd picture the scenario where my parents would get deported at work and coming home to no one, for it to happen while I was at school. That was something that really traumatized me as I was growing up."

Victor Gallardo-Molina (known for his willingness to jump in to help, his great care for his community, and his understated but clear and hard-earned confidence in his own skin) offered his voice on this as well, "Every day we live in fear. Every day my parents go to work and there's always the idea in the back of the head that today ICE[25] might just drop into work and just start checking everybody. And so, they come back home and we're good for the day. But at 5am, 3am, 4am, whatever time they leave to work the next day, I'm pretty sure the fear is back on and it's on full. And they go to work eight, nine, ten hours a day and my mom works twelve hour days sometimes six days a week. So you know, you take that into consideration, six out of the seven days a week, she's probably thinking about the fact that any day now ICE could just drop by her job and start taking people. And I think her main concern is: What's going to happen to me? What's going to happen to my brothers? I hate having the conversation with her about it because she's always like, 'Hey, if I ever get taken by ICE, I need you to take care of your brothers.' And I'm always like, 'yeah, obviously, I'm not going to leave them.' But sometimes I think about it and the fact that she really means it. Every time she talks about it, she knows that I know, but she knows what kind of a possibility and a reality that could be and she wants to keep reminding me." [Hear more about Victor's story at www.loveinatimeoffear.com and click on the video of Victor.]

Montse, remembering similar experiences, adds, "It makes you stronger, though, at the same time. And decisive, like I need to build an action plan to protect my siblings. And yet," she continues, "if that were to happen, I'd probably be a mess."

Everyone pauses to recognize that there are pieces of themselves that they value that have grown out of these experiences. But that does not justify them or make what they have gone through okay.

And the anxiety is not in isolated moments. As Andy adds, "honestly, it's always there."

Nelly (a student leader with a humble, deeply respecting and nurturing demeanor, great warmth, and a quiet power), thoughtfully listening to most of the conversation up to this point, gently interjects, "I stand in a very different spot. I'm not undocumented but receive a lot of the messages

---

25. ICE is shorthand for Immigration and Customs Enforcement.

others get. I don't think I can even understand. People say 'I understand' a lot but you can't. That word is not appropriate if you're not in their position. You can say, 'I hear you, I'm listening to you,' I can even see a little bit but never can I understand if I'm not directly affected. I try to be very careful with the words that I say because they're very delicate with someone who is undocumented." She continues, "It's a blessing that I don't have to worry about having this fear of being stopped. I feel like as a citizen I have a big privilege in where I decide to work and the power I'm given because of my legal status, like voting and being involved with policy and all of that. It's like a good decent pressure to exercise that privilege that I have."

Recognizing that there are things we simply do not and cannot understand seems to be another way of showing love. It is not the end game. But it is a doorway, realizing that we don't know, creating some room to learn what we don't know, to hear from someone else what life is like for them, and then believing them, and from that point on, refusing to let our own experiences be the only litmus test for understanding or truth.

Andy jumps in thinking about the issue at large and the racial, class, and economic dynamics at play. "Our people have definitely been given the short end of the stick and I think it's hard to prosper in a system that has been designed for us not to prosper. It's hard because my people are really hardworking. How do you stay positive when everything is so connected? People are really creative and innovative, they'll do whatever will work. And coming here with the fear that it all can be taken away, how can we access resources? It keeps some of us who could be really powerful in this nation be pushed aside and be subdued."

Fear is big. It is an enemy and major inhibitor of love. It sometimes inhibits even just the basic ability to breathe.

Veronica chimes in, "My dad is a resident and my mom is a citizen. But despite the fact that my mom is a citizen, she's still afraid that someone might take away her citizenship."

In this statement, Veronica is identifying that even those people who are legally a part of this nation—citizens, at home here—are made to feel that they do not belong. The messages they absorb is that they are still not welcome and never will be. They are gripped by fear that they could be kicked out of their home any minute because of the associations with the color of their skin. When this is the reality, is it really the law that is at base here?

Veronica continues, "My dad is a resident but he's afraid that he might not be able to renew in the next two years. There's always this fear. And it feels like it'll never go away . . . We have created so much here. This place has made us into the people we are today and the fact that we have to keep fighting to prove that we belong here, whether documented or not, is exhausting. It also shows the unloving part." Veronica is a US citizen. She still experiences this.

When you don't feel welcome, you don't feel safe. When you don't feel safe, you don't feel loved. Fighting to prove you belong is exhausting.

Reflecting on the key questions again, the conversation deepens around recognizing that their experiences are marked by privileges even as they are also marked by significant struggles. Talk floats to ideas of their parents.

Montse reflects, "We're also privileged because we're educated and have come to college. We access the language and structures. What would love look like to our parents or others who don't have access to this conversation?"

Nelly adds, "Sometimes I try so hard to make my parents understand but they're like, 'they're not bad people, they don't know what they're doing,' because my parents are just good people and are unwilling to see any type of evil or bad intentions. They're like, 'Nelly, don't be so negative.' But I'm not trying to be negative, the system is just so negative."

Veronica adds, "They're always looking at the positive, which is sometimes annoying." The whole room erupts into laughter. "They're so compassionate," Veronica continues with a smirk on her face and an incredibly deep respect apparent in her demeanor and underlying every word as she talks about her parents.

I asked if they had any clues as to how their parents might answer that question of what feels like love to them right now.

Victor offers, "My first instinct is to always say, it's not my fault that I'm illegal. It's something you grow up labeled as. I know who I am. And I feel like I'm American." But, he continues, "people are always looking for somebody to blame and if I say it's not my fault, they're going to hit me with, 'okay, who's fault is it' and at that point I can't throw my parents under the bus and say, 'well my parents brought me in,' because that's like putting the blame on them and that's not something I want to do. So it's kind of a tricky thing."

Every one of the students spoke of their parents with deep respect, recognizing the difficult decisions they have made and continue to make. They also shared the grief of what has been lost. Victor tells the story of the opportunity that DACA allowed him to travel back to see family in Mexico once as his grandma was dying. "I was there on my grandma's deathbed and all I could think of was how hard I wished that instead of me being there, it was my mom. And my mom was the youngest one out of fifteen. And she was the only one that my grandma hadn't seen before she died. I thought about what my mom would do to be there in that moment just to hug her. It was something I knew would never happen and it was heartbreaking."

Blanca offers some thoughts to that. "What gets in the way of our parents seeing what we see is my mom's faith." She [her mom] thinks, "It'll be okay. God will provide. Things happen for a reason. We can overcome." Everyone makes agreeing sounds. Blanca continues, "and as much as yes, I agree with her, it's also hard to only see things from that perspective that faith will carry us through it all because we see how ugly the systems are and how bad it is." There seems to be an agreement in the room that faith continues to be an important staple for their parents, a source of strength and hope, and perhaps even self-protection in the midst of circumstances of great risk and loss. There is a question about whether or not those statements of faith both provide needed strength and also potentially mask some of the realities.

It is ironic and, perhaps painful, that these same messages are messages held by some of the groups, as indicated above, who are against welcoming immigrants into the US. I think about how people on multiple sides use these messages, "Things happen for a reason." "God is still in control." Sometimes communities are using these messages as a way of comfort when it feels like the walls are coming down all around them or perhaps are being built between them and their family in another place. I wonder if sometimes other communities are using these messages as a way to not have to take responsibility for some of the implications of the decisions that they participate in. When are these messages in service to ideas of a God that does not care about issues of systemic injustice but only about a narrowed personalized faith (we'll explore this a bit more in chapter 5)? When are these messages in service to ideas of a God that is with us when we are experiencing injustice and giving us strength to fight for a different world?

Montse picks up where Blanca left off. "I've started to have a lot more issues identifying myself as a Christian when a lot of the rejection and a lot of the hate comes from people in the same group. It's so strange. And at the same time my parents are talking about how everything will be okay because God will make a way. It's so hard to not become resentful."

The struggle comes in identifying with a faith that has been so important to her and her family and that also seems to be one of the reasons that so many people are against her and her family's ability to stay in the US.

Andy continues the conversation, "How can people put oppression on people while also saying they believe and that they are being 'a good Christian'? People can either be Christian or take the title of Christian but not do it. I think a lot of people turn to the Bible and the message is there but people take their own adaptation or their own understanding to suit whatever situation they're in."

We let that sink in. It rings true around the table. Then, "Speaking of labels," I ask, "how do you want people to think of you?"

Andy starts, "I've thought about this a lot. If I wanted to define myself, I'd say I am a hardworking, very family oriented, loving person. I feel like a lot of people see me at a very surface level. 'He's a Mexican or Hispanic or Latinx or the smart guy or whatever'" and believe the messages they hear about those things.

Andy starts a story to illustrate his point, "I was in high school and I always pushed myself to be the best I could be and so I was in an advanced math class and obviously the population was staggered toward people who are not Hispanic. I was the only Mexican person in the class. It came down to classmates asking me what I was and when I said Mexican they said, 'No, there's no way. You must be Indian and your dad probably works at Intel' and when I asked them why they said that they said, 'Oh because Mexicans aren't smart.'" Andy pauses, "If you cut people off at the root you can't expect them to grow and be in a position to show off their intelligence. From that point on, I've always wanted to prove those people wrong and that there is a way to be intelligent and chase our dreams and do what we want to do. We have no resources, so the issue is bigger than just that. That's something I wish I could change and want to help change in the future. I want to go back and empower others to know that they can do it."

Veronica goes next, "I identify myself as a woman who is consistently fighting for her loved ones and the community trying to provide a safe place for them and make them feel validated and that they belong and are worth the investment. I want to make that my life goal. I feel like I'm trying to achieve that. No matter what happens, I'll always be at the front lines fighting for them whether it's policy or with my little sister's teacher asking why he's being rude, or whether it's questioning authority or whatever or just providing my home, opening my doors to everyone. I just want to be that person that makes people feel that they're valued."

Blanca adds her voice, "family oriented. Family is one of the most important things. Also I really value my education and the opportunity to get an education. I'm helping others. I see myself as someone who tries to do that in different ways, if it's on homework or giving words of encouragement to others or serving the community in different forms. I think one of the messages that is often said, especially of Latinas in the community, is they're not really seen in those positions of having authority and power, especially in the world of politics and policy. So, I see myself as someone who has the ability to do that. I think that part of it is culturally. In Mexican culture, women don't often get the opportunity to be as strong as they are or have as strong of a presence or dominant force in whatever they do. Sometimes they are taken advantage of or are easy targets. I see myself as someone who is trying to go against that."

A WAY FORWARD

As we wrap up our conversation, I take a deep breath in gratitude for the power and pain shared around the table. I feel lucky to be in that place, invited to hear these stories, and that they have made room for me at their table. What does not feel like love to those voices above are actions and words that communicate unwelcome, that reduce, deflect, or dehumanize (e.g. the term "illegals"). It does not feel like love when someone rests on the privilege to not have to know or to not consider the implications of our actions on our immigrant neighbors. It does not feel like love to ask them to do our hard work for us (physically, emotionally, or spiritually).

What does feel like love seems to land in three major categories to begin with (we will unpack these even further in later chapters):

- Love feels like the expression of real compassion. In other words, a listening and caring presence, feeling someone else's story and circumstances, restoring human-ness and dignity and safety in relationship in the process. Love in this sense is an actual curiosity, a desire to know, accepting the risk to hear hard things and an openness to learn to love our immigrant neighbors. It is showing up with open ears. And this is just a start.

- To feel like love this compassion needs to be coupled with serious reflection. Our immigrant neighbors are asking us to thoughtfully consider how our own choices and life circumstances are different from theirs, ask why those are different, how we benefit from privilege and/or where we share struggle, and how we might be complicit in participating in the conditions that have created the circumstances of struggle or opportunity for them. This work helps us to love "bigger," as Montse calls us. It asks us to consider the systems we are a part of and how these systems are harder for some to navigate through no fault of their own. For a simple example, if you are the first person in your family to apply to college, how are you to know how to fill out all of the paperwork, what to turn in when, and how to navigate the stages of the process? People who have family members who have already navigated these processes (sometimes for generations) have an advantage. That advantage does not mean they are more "fit" for college. It does mean that getting there might be easier. Love considers these dynamics. This, too, is part of the process.

- To feel like love, compassion and reflection also need concrete action in relationship. This is not transactional action where we write a check or donate something and call it good. Those kinds of acts of charity or mercy can help as a starting point or in a moment of crisis or emergency. After all, we did hear real concrete needs. However, the meeting of a need with a gift communicates love when concrete actions come out of the knowing that is a part of being in relationship with someone. That knowing also makes it more likely that the gift will meet an actual need. In relationship that does not feel like charity. In relationship, it does not feel like one-way giving. In relationship, it feels like the love of someone who cares for someone who knows they are cared about. It also means there is a reciprocity in the giving and receiving.

The three together are important. It is not enough to empathize with someone's story and get a type of emotional high off of it. If it doesn't lead to action, it doesn't feel like love. If someone is in a burning building and we stop to feel what they must be feeling, even if it moves us to feeling compassion and care, if we then continue walking down the street without taking action to help them, that does not communicate love. Love feels like helping them get out of the building. This may require putting our body or our resources on the line. Love feels like halting the continuation of trauma. It feels like sitting with them so that they are not alone while they process what they just survived. Love feels like making sure they have a place to sleep, something to eat, and someone to stay with them that night and those to come. Love doesn't walk away. It acts.

Our immigrant neighbors in this chapter have told us that often what communicates love are practical, sometimes simple actions out of a knowing and sustained relationship. At the heart of this is not only providing goods, it is removing a sense of real insecurity. It is soothing a measure of sustained and gripping fear and unknowing that is an ever-present companion of many of our immigrant neighbors. When practical love is offered out of a relationship of mutuality, it offers back a measure of dignity to our immigrant neighbors countering the messages that they often hear to the contrary. It also re-humanizes all of us.

But love is not always simple. The three together also recognize that the conditions of need are both personal and systemic and the reality is that our immigrant neighbors are facing systems that sometimes make even the most basic parts of life incredibly difficult, including the basic ability of being together with one's family members. As I write, more than a hundred men, many asylum seekers, are being detained in a federal prison a mere seventy-five minute drive away from my house. Separated from their families, they have been denied medical care, phone calls, and access to lawyers and clergy, basic provisions that are usually granted within prisons of all kinds all over our country.[26] This weekend I joined with hundreds of people from Christian, Sikh, and Jewish communities and neighbors of various other faiths or no faith at all to hold religious services right outside the barbed wire of the prison grounds so that the men inside might hear. Some held flags outside their windows telling us of their homes. They were humans reaching out to other humans wondering if someone might make room for them.

As people of faith wanting to care for our immigrant neighbors, we need the courage to ask ourselves some difficult questions of what it is that we hope for in this world. What do we hope and desire for ourselves? What do we extend as rights and hopes for others? What do we have the will to decide to be and do? As Ada María Isasi-Díaz reminds us, "Decisions are a

26. Wilson, "Detainees in Oregon."

taking hold of understandings and desires and translating them into action . . . we never choose what we do not desire."[27]

In these stories, we clearly see a situation where our fears have created significant fear for our immigrant neighbors. Few of us know what it is like to live every single day wondering if our families will be in tact by the end of the day. This is not imagined fear. It is a fear that came true for one of my students this year as her father was deported mere weeks before her wedding. It is a fear that came true for someone in my friend's church who has been in a detention facility for months now away from his three children, leaving his wife without an income to pay the rent. It is a fear coming true for thousands of families at our border and in detention centers today. These realities are not new. Families were separated in the Trail of Tears, in the period of slavery, in Japanese incarceration/internment camps. It is not new. It is also not okay. As people of faith, we cannot continue to claim "family values" while supporting policies that separate immigrant families or that delay the reuniting of those families. Otherwise, we need to be prepared to honestly answer the question: Whose families do we value? It has been forty days since the president signed his executive order on family separation. We will keep counting the days and showing up until families are back together.

There have been parts of Gimena's story and Erendira's and Montse's and Andy's and Blanca's and Victor's and Nelly's and Veronica's and the eleven million others that are simply not fair. They cause me to rage and to weep. They should. I cry out for the sins of our ways of being in the world that have communicated that there is no room for them in our neighborhoods or at our tables. The world that we have inherited has not favored us all the same.

But the world that we have inherited does not have to be the world that we leave behind.

27. Isasi-Díaz, *La Lucha Continues*, 190.

3

You Don't Know What Kind of Courage It Takes

Bridging Gaps, Shouldering Responsibility, and Being a Muslim in the US Today

MOST SATURDAY AFTERNOONS YOU can find my friend Harris Zafar at a local mall with a friend or two, a sign and/or t-shirt that says "Talk to a Muslim," and coffee and cake. I don't particularly like cake. But I love the rest of it. It is part of Harris's efforts to shrink the number of US Americans who report that they have never knowingly met a Muslim—a number that a Pew Research Center survey reports in recent years as 62 percent.[1]

I have made it part of my own work to join in that process by making sure that all of my students have an opportunity to engage with Harris or one of my other friends within the Muslim community. I do this because there is a lot of fear around Islam in a post-9/11 world where we have no shortage of messages about ISIS, radical Islam, terror, etc. I also do it because Harris is just so drat awesome.

THE FRAME

As with the other communities represented in this text, the engagement of Muslim neighbors by other faith communities, especially Christian faith

1. Lipka, "How Many People of Different Faiths Do You Know?"

communities, has been complicated. Responses have included outright war, persecution, and/or exclusion, often fueled by casting the Muslim "other" as evil or at least on the other side of the truth. At other times, the experience of Christian communities has been desired separation out of theological understandings of holiness that seem to indicate the need to not associate with "the unclean" or "unholy" or fear that all Muslims might try to convert them to Islam. Still others have resisted both of these messages and approaches in order to embrace our Muslim neighbors as religious cousins, recognizing Islam as a part of the Abrahamic faiths that trace their roots to Abraham in the Jewish, Muslim, and Christian scriptures.

This complicated spectrum has been present within US history in some potentially unique ways. The narrative of the American colonies being founded (in part) for freedom to practice religion, particularly those branches of religion that were persecuted in Europe, embedded deep in the US psyche, although in paradoxical ways. Some interpreted that to mean that there was enough land for everyone to go and make their own colonies with their own religion and, therefore, people could leave me alone to practice the one I want. Other spaces became known as refuges for a variety of religious orientations (still predominantly Christian). The paradoxical identity of understanding the American colonies to be "a city on a hill" or a "light to the nations" further complicated these practices in reality. Some of our ancestors understood this to mean that the US had/has a special relationship with the divine as creating a type of kingdom of God on Earth and, therefore, in order to maintain that special relationship, we have to maintain our Christian roots and identity in a specific and majority way. However, the US has also billed a "freedom of religion" that, at least theoretically, is extended to those outside of Christianity. This has raised the question throughout US history: Is our "city on a hill-ness" a reflection of a particular Christian identity? Is it a reflection of our ability to welcome, embrace, live alongside, and be changed by and with others with different beliefs and practices? Does it exist at all?[2]

As is often the case, theological understandings of human-ness have been entangled in sorting out our responses to these questions. Our ancestors asked questions about what it means to be human, especially if being human is to be created in the image of God. This becomes particularly crucial when they were unsure as to whether or not the God of Christian

2. To explore this more in a summary fashion, see the PBS documentary film, *God in America*.

scripture, history, and experience is the same as the God of Judaism or Islam. The way they answered those questions had significant implications for how they would see their neighbors of other faiths. And at no point were these questions entirely separated from economic interests, social dynamics, and other systems that make up human life in community.

Sometimes our ancestors recognized the full human-ness of those practicing other religions from their own. At other times, they developed theological answers to their questions reflecting "the fundamental belief that human dignity is not inherent, that it is only conferred upon conversion."[3] This belief extended to enslaved Africans, to many people indigenous to the Americas, and to others with belief systems outside of traditional Christianity. And in each case, it raised further complicated implications. If one converted, could they no longer be enslaved? If one converted, should they then be considered a full and equal participant in all the rights and privileges of the community? The ways our ancestors answered these questions often revealed that the full humanity and life abundance of the othered neighbor was not of primary concern.

These theological acrobatics about defining human-ness have been harmful and they have been untrue. As Mae Elise Cannon, Lisa Sharon Harper, Troy Jackson, and Soong-Chan Rah boldly state in their collaborative text, *Forgive Us: Confessions of a Compromised Faith*, "One does not have to convert to become human according to Scripture."[4] Plain and simple. We are created human by birth, not by new-birth.

But that has not always been how our ancestors saw it. And their eyes were clouded by different understandings of what a holy life was marked by as well. Some held notions of holiness as separation from anything that might make them "dirty" or risk their own "purity." This sometimes translated into fear and avoidance of certain "types" of people known for being somehow "unclean."[5] It also often ignored the social, cultural, and economic dynamics that impacted the theological understandings of what was defined as "dirty" or "clean." It meant that any interactions with the "unholy other" had to be transactional in particular ways and brief. Separation became the norm under the guise of protection.

I still see evidence of this understanding of holiness show up when I teach Religions of the World at a Christ-centered university. I take an

---

3. Cannon, et al., "Forgive Us," 194.

4. Ibid., 197.

5. See more about this in Trentaz, *Theology in the Age of Global AIDS & HIV.*

interfaith and experiential approach in that class where students have opportunities to gain appreciative knowledge of other faith traditions, as well as their own if they have one, and do so by learning directly and face-to-face with some of our neighbors in addition to the academic approach to comparative religions and exploring recent news articles. Some students come hungry to learn. Some come completely indifferent because they have not seen much point to religion in their lives. Some students come into the class full of fear around engaging religion at all, due to the ways they have been hurt by organized religion. And some come in full of fear of damaging their faith by learning about other faiths. Often, students bring a mix of multiple orientations to the class.

What I see, after fifteen weeks of engaging with our neighbors and learning about what they hold to be sacred, is that the fear in the room diminishes and respect increases. This feels consistent to me with the way of Jesus. Jesus did not shame and exclude those who were othered by the dominant religious system of the day. He sat with and got to know them so that he could show them love in a way that counted. He also did not completely throw away his religious tradition and roots but worked to call his community back to the core of love of God, self, and other (even if that other was deemed an enemy in his time or ours).

It is clear that Muslim Americans are one of those othered in our time. In *This Muslim American Life: Dispatches from the War on Terror*, Moustafa Bayoumi quotes Edward Said when he says: "Malicious generalizations about Islam have become the last acceptable form of denigration of foreign culture in the West; what is said about the Muslim mind, or character, or religion, or culture as a whole cannot now be said in mainstream discussion about Africans, Jews, other Orientals, or Asians."[6] This was in October 1996. Pre-9/11. Pre-"War on Terror." Said could see the dynamics brewing.

The ways that Muslims are talked about in this country do not only shape Muslims, they shape the rest of us as well. Bayoumi discusses the impacts of what he calls "War on Terror Culture" on international law as well as effects on "the national psyche." Things we had "previously considered illegal (even if we condoned) such things as targeted killings, indefinite detention without trial, and torture. Now these actions are not only condoned but generally accepted as necessary and prudent, and they are frequently portrayed as such on television and in the movies."[7] Things we might have

6. Bayoumi, *This Muslim American Life,* 254.

7. Ibid., 255.

grieved, in other times, become things we look away from or even justify. Fear is definitely alive here. It looms large and seems insatiable.

As people of faith, we need to ask critical questions regarding how much our own sense of security is compatible with a gospel that reaches across international borders and how our love for our neighbors extends to those who practice a different religion. Many of our fears have been codified in policies of "national security." In those processes, have we also considered the broader context that has created the conditions of "us" verses "them" regarding the US and, seemingly, the whole Muslim world? Immediately after 9/11, President George W. Bush was careful to remind the US American people that we are not at war with Islam. And yet, not everyone seems to have gotten that message. So where do our fears serve to keep us safe? And where do our fears serve to create conditions of harm for people, created in the image of God, practicing a religion that is other than our own? Where, is our own fear, impacted by "War on Terror Culture," creating a different kind of terror for our Muslim neighbors?

Bayoumi talks about the concept of "guilt by association," that marks many Muslims, especially young men. He states, it is "as if all males of that age ['MAMs' military-aged males] are reducible (and thus justifiably killed due) to their potential for terrorism."[8] Yet, young white males continue to perpetrate acts of domestic terrorism and do not receive the same kind of guilt by association. There are many questions to raise here. What kind of impact does this type of categorization or profiling have on our Muslim neighbors? Bayoumi continues, "This idea that you are seen not as a complex human being but only as a purveyor of possible future violence illustrates the extraordinary predicament of the heart of contemporary Muslim American life. To be Muslim American today is to be full of potential, and not in the sweet way that grandmothers and elementary school teachers use the word."[9]

Policies are made in fearful anticipation of what might be possible, viewing entire communities with suspicion. That is a problem for faith communities that believe in love and justice. As Bayoumi reminds us, "'Muslim' is not a synonym for 'terrorist.'"[10]

As we discussed in chapter 2, violence is a serious issue for concern in our country today. We cannot ignore this. However, we need to be diligent

8. Ibid., 9.

9. Ibid.

10. Ibid., 10.

to consider the actual roots of that violence rather than finding an easy scapegoat to tack it onto, thereby potentially missing our opportunities to legitimately address the problem. Where has the image of the "Muslim terrorist" been used too quickly to find someone to blame? What are the implications both for our real understanding of how to make our world safe for our children to grow up in and what are the implications for entire communities of our Muslim neighbors who absorb our often misplaced and inappropriately spread-out fears?

The question of how to address those Muslims who have taken an extremist view is a question of concern as much (if not more) within Muslim communities themselves as it is for those outside of Muslim communities. For those of us who are not Muslim, it raises confusion as to what we know about Islam. For our Muslim neighbors, it creates the need to separate themselves from those promoting violent extremism as well as to communicate the good and beautiful core of what they find sacred.

For all of us loom questions about how and where we draw boundaries and identity. Bayoumi quotes Palestinian filmmaker, Hany Abu-Assad, responding to a question about whether he believed in nationalism for Palestine. Bayoumi says, "his answer is instructive beyond the particularities of the Palestinian struggle and can be generalized to suggest a way of escaping the violent gridlock of the War on Terror." In his response, Abu-Assad states:

> Nationalism is about having or wanting a country, with its own national identity . . . Right now, I don't care about "country." I care about civil rights, human rights, equal opportunity, justice; I don't care about whether you are Palestinian or Christian or Muslim or Jewish. These are individual identities that are not necessary to share with others. What you share with others is your values, whatever god you want, have different opinions about everything, but our values should still be about respecting each other's equality and civil rights.[11]

I know for many faith communities, it is not easy to hear and not easy to say that we do not care about whether or not someone is Christian or Jewish or Muslim. Many of us care deeply because what we have experienced has been life-giving and we want to share that source of life with others. We have even been told that sharing it is our responsibility. Yet sometimes there are also arrogant notions of "right" and "wrong" that

11. Ibid., 257.

interfere in that sharing. When they do, I have seen time and time again that this desire to share something life-giving with others results in exclusion rather than life. Sometimes our feelings of certainty mean that we do not listen very well to our neighbors. We do not take the time to learn what they care about, what they find sacred, and how they practice it. So we accidentally (or intentionally) desacralize what gives them life. It does not have to be like this. Abu-Assad is suggesting that we might be at a moment when we need to strip down to some basics—human to human—before building back up regarding the identities that make up our particular and different ways of being human.

I remember one semester in a constructive theology class I asked my students the question: What was Jesus's point? Was Jesus, Jesus's point? Or did he have a different point? We were beginning to engage ideas and questions about the kingdom or kin-dom of God, something that, as one of my students came to recognize, "Jesus couldn't shut up about." This is, indeed, central to Jesus's message, ministry, and methods in the world: Shalom— right relationship, justice, life-giving love, peace, wellness, full aliveness and flourishing. This is what the great loves are calling us toward.

In engaging our neighbors of other faiths we can take our cues from the kin-dom of God that says that good relationship is a key to abundant life. As we have already discussed, Jesus was a boundary-crosser. He did not see those who were outside of dominant religious practices in his community as untouchable. He sought them out and spent time with them. He recognized what they had to offer the whole. He showed them that God loves them. He demonstrated his own holiness by being with those who had been deemed unholy by the religious structures of his day. In doing so, he did not say that we should do away with the whole of religion as we knew it. Rather, he called people back to the core of what it meant to be people of God and pointed out (sometimes gently, sometimes fiercely) where we had gotten too nearsighted about some things and had forgotten the core of God's heart for the hurt and the excluded. He reminded people that God is the creator of *all* people. This includes our neighbors of other faiths. So how do we show love, in the midst of these heated dynamics, to our Muslim neighbors?

THE CONVERSATIONS

Recognizing the complexities of Muslim experience in the US, I sat down with several of my Muslim friends, neighbors, and students to talk about their experiences. I heard powerful stories of help, troubling stories of harm or dismissal, and was reminded of the inspiring strength and faith of Muslim communities.

Before we get to those voices, though, it might be helpful to start with some basics. Islam is the name of the religion. Muslim is one who practices the religion of Islam. The Qur'an is the name of Muslims' holy scripture. Allah is the Arabic name for God. Muhammad is the name of the prophet to whom God revealed God's word (as written down in the Qur'an) through the Angel Gabriel. Muslims pray five times a day, 365 days a year. The masjid/mosque is the place where the community gathers for collective prayers. It also sometimes serves as a place for other community gatherings.

A few more basics, as summarized by Paul M. Barrett in *American Islam*, are:

> Two-thirds of American Muslims are immigrants; one third, native born. Most American Muslims are not Arab, and most Americans of Arab descent are Christian, not Muslim. People of South Asian descent—those with roots in Pakistan, India, Bangladesh, and Afghanistan—make up 34 percent of American Muslims, according to the polling organization Zogby International. Arab-Americans constitute only 26 percent, while another 20 percent are native-born American blacks, most of whom are converts. The remaining 20 percent come from Africa, Iran, Turkey, and elsewhere.

> . . . some beliefs and practices vary depending on region and sect. In America, Muslims do not think and act alike any more than Christians do. That said, all observant Muslims acknowledge Islam's "five pillars": faith in one God, prayer, charity, fasting during Ramadan, and pilgrimage to Mecca. Muslims are also united in the way they pray. The basic choreography of crossing arms, bowing, kneeling, and prostrating oneself is more or less the same in mosques everywhere.[12]

The people I talked to all currently live in the US but have formerly lived in Pakistan, Dubai (United Arab Emirates), Saudi Arabia, England,

---

12. Barrett, *American Islam*, 6–7.

Canada, Switzerland, the Dominican Republic, Bosnia, and US cities of New York, Chicago, Miami, Phoenix, Sacramento, Nashville, and Portland, among others. They identify as Pakistani, Mexican, Bosnian, and Ethiopian. They range in age from their early 20s to nearly 50. Every one of them holds enduring understandings of their faith, often differing in practice and emphasis from each other. Their diversity is an important reminder of the diversity of the Islamic faith and the Muslim communities in the US.

Arman Butt (relaxed but confident, a PhD in Bioengineering, the youth leader at his local mosque with a heart to serve those in need in his city and to help young people also nurture this heart, a loving father and husband, demonstrating this as he rocked his teething one-year old daughter while speaking with me in the lovely home he shares with his wife, Nairyna) speaks both of this diversity as well as the perceptions of its nonexistence. "I think what generally Americans see is that Islam is a singular unit and everybody is either bad or good or everyone follows the same religion, but if you know anything about Islam, there are, I think, at least 73 sects, generally divided between Sunni and Shia." Arman and Nairyna belong to one of those sects that is receiving negative pressure not only in general, but their community is also significantly persecuted by other Muslim sects in many parts of the world. Speaking of fear, the anxiety regarding needing to face this additional layer of potential harm, "affords us different concerns than just being a practicing Muslim," Arman adds. The realities of US Muslims are not singular. The dynamics are as unique as each person and each family experience.

Nairyna Constantino (Arman's wife and mother of two young children, also with a degree in engineering, a convert to Islam who was raised in a Mexican Catholic family, patient and strong and still clearly impacted by the divisions and misunderstandings within her family) recounts when she and Arman first got together, "it was very difficult to bring up to my family that I had a Muslim boyfriend. They were like, 'terrorist!' That was their first reaction." She goes on to recount that her grandma actually asked him directly if he was a terrorist and that her family asked if she was going to be "one of his five wives."

The tension did not stop after they got to know Arman. "Even after seven years, they still make those comments." Nairyna talks about how her family has referred to their denomination's conventions as "terrorist conventions." "It's so stressful," Nairyna adds, especially as this was on top of her own adjustment to the "different cultural and religious practices" of

Islam after her conversion. "No matter what it is, my family has opinions on everything. And they always tie it to me taking my children's freedoms away. I have a brother who is atheist and they look at him and me and it's like they'd rather be like him than me." She tells of moments that particularly sting, "my mom had cancer this last year and had surgery and my daughter was a couple of months old. Travelling would be difficult and I said I would come later when she was recovering and her response was, 'you people,'" Nairyna pauses, "'you Muslims claim to want to help other people in need but you don't even help your own family in need.'" The feeling Nairyna gets is that "I either abandoned or betrayed them, I don't know." Yet, she takes it with patience, even though it is hard. "In Islam, you don't have to retaliate or talk back," Nairyna continues, "just respect them and God will take care of that other side, which is hard because we're human" and hard because she is stuck between two sides of her family.

These tensions are on top of tensions Arman experiences simply living as a Muslim man in the US. "I would consider myself born again, kind of," Arman offers, recognizing that is terminology often associated with Christianity, but indicating his own "conversion-type" of experience to become more serious about the religion he was raised in. He talks about that seriousness coinciding with deciding to get married to Nairyna. Along with it came some of the typical "markers" of Islam. "They [Nairyna's family] especially didn't like it when I started growing out my beard. In Chicago, everyone is clean-shaven usually. On the North side, I would get 'the looks,' but on the South side, I would get respect. The African American community, they have an understanding of Islam."

Sameya Amme's family reflects some of the African Muslim experience. Sameya is a political science major with a spit-fire passion to bring justice into the world and an easy, although still feisty, laugh. She is a first-generation US born African American woman embodying the tension between dominant US and her family's cultural worldviews and, as such, serves as a trailblazer and bridge. She tells about her family's experience of fleeing persecution and violence in their home country, leaving Ethiopia through Somalia and Kenya (both places also experiencing violence at the time) before seeking refuge in the US. "Even to this day my people are hunted down in the streets, at their colleges, thrown off buildings, massacred in large numbers and you never hear about these things in the news. Are they forgotten still to this day? Hopefully I can still bring a voice to that." [See more about Sameya at www.loveinatimeoffear.com and click on the video of Sameya.]

Sameya was born a year after her mom came to the US. She talks about the risks her parents took, especially her father. "In refugee families, there's this big stigma. I don't want to let my parents down," she recounts. "All of his heartache. I'm sitting here in my own apartment with a full ride scholarship to college." And she states and seems to question at the same time, "It was all worth it." Sameya talks about how they don't talk about emotions in her family, about how her parents want to go back, how they miss their home, but that the community is not the same anymore. These realities and their direct impact on her family is part of why Sameya has chosen to study political science, something that her father brags about.

For all of the people I spoke with, family and faith communities are incredibly important.

Sahar Ahsan (an endearing woman with a wise and gentle confidence who exudes patience and thoughtfulness, a mother of three, shaped by a significant global perspective in her growing up and adult years) remembers, "The bulk of my being raised was in the Middle East and I was pretty much in an Islamic environment." But in her school, she recounts, "I grew up basically around kids of every different background. I was around Syrian kids, Palestinian kids, Lebanese kids, European kids. It was almost like a little global village just within our school. Not all were Muslims, some were from other religious backgrounds, but never did I face any kind of hatred. Everybody seemed to get along pretty well, so I almost grew up not really knowing what hatred or anything of that was, living in Saudi Arabia." She talks about how her family's mix of "liberalism and conservativism" allowed her to engage in gatherings of mixed company with her parents present and to participate in sports growing up, which was not the reality for all of her friends. "And I can remember from a very young age," Sahar continues, "that I was still able to vocalize what my boundaries were and even then I didn't face any kind of hatred. In fact, the opposite, I would always get respect back from all the students who really cared."

She talks about moving to England in high school and continuing to practice identifying her own values and boundaries and resisting the normal pressures of teenage years and then moving to Canada to attend university. She recounts the continuation of a feeling of being in a global village while maintaining strong roots in her community. "There was always a connection to the community and people outside of the community."

Both Sahar and her conversation partner, Nasreen Farouq (witty, honest, sure of herself, holding degrees in both interior design and medicine, a recent empty-nester along with her husband, and who describes herself as "a gypsy at heart"), begin by identifying that they have largely had positive experiences while living in the US. And yet, they are hesitant to use their real names because of the fear associated with the "rhetoric" in the US right now. I ask about this dynamic, wondering if it is simply that this rhetoric is not new to them so they are already resourced to be able to deflect it or if they are tired of naming it or something else altogether.

Nasreen responds, "I would say that our community is more equipped because of our motto [the motto shared by their sect of Islam] of: Love for All, Hatred for None. We don't believe in violence and we don't believe in any kind of response in an aggressive way and our response has always been with love and with dialogue." This is a posture taken and affirmed by many of these neighbors.

Sahar continues, this motto "is worldwide and is not from today but is actually from many, many, many years prior, from the founder of the community. I think the community in general tries to live up to those words in every form of our life, in our day to day life, within our community, outside of our community, at work, at school. We strive. We may not be perfect at it, but we continue to believe in it and affirm it. It is part of our pledge that we will do justice for our nation, that we will do justice for the people around us. We take this pledge every time we meet. It is a constant reminder that love is for all and hatred for none. And when it comes to people of every kind of religion, every background, the belief that we hold strong is humanity first. We may defer from them, but we don't have the right to call them wrong or to say that because they're not following our path or religion that we don't accept them. We should try to bring people closer, not divide them."

Nasreen states, "We're a peace-loving community. Basically, wherever we are, we try to promote the true teachings of Islam. Loving thy neighbor is a very big thing. And our current khalifa says that our neighbor is not just your next door neighbor, it's actually forty houses down your block. The whole block you should be worried about and if one of your neighbors goes to bed hungry, then you'll be asked on the day of judgment, what did you do to help that neighbor? Islam talks about that a lot. If you cook something, we always share with our neighbors. If you take something, they automatically feel less threatened. We should always take the initiative because the parties who are scared of us as Muslims don't know who we are and the responsibility falls on us."

I confess that I am uncomfortable with that statement. In my white, middle-class, US American ears, it both makes sense and does not sound fair for the Muslim community to shoulder the additional burden and responsibility of healing rifts or removing fear. I point this out and ask what people think about that.

Nairyna responds, "It's not fair, but we do it because it's the right thing to do. We don't want people to form an opinion on us just because they're ignorant, so if we can help, then why not have their heart be softer by our interaction rather than hate us?"

Nasreen and Sahar talk a lot about creating possibilities for dialogue. Arman mentions the emphasis on interfaith programs, outreach programs, and public engagement.

Arman continues, "Protesting is not allowed. Anything that disrupts the way of life of others, especially blocking streets and businesses. We say the power of the pen is very powerful. We use editorials, op-eds, we have a national team that deals with PR and puts out press releases condemning terrorist attacks, but we are not the type of community that gets in peoples' faces."

He tells the story of someone who "while drunk shot up one of our mosques" in Connecticut. "Instead of us testifying against him, we engaged with him and now he's a regular visitor. We tried to get the judge to be lenient on the sentence because we knew that he knew what he did was wrong. Now he engages with that community there. That's the kind of experience we want people to have with us."

Arman also takes a more theological approach, talking about a moment when a leader was speaking to the community and reflecting on "what [it would] take for God to accept us as is. To put away arrogance and pride. When we put that away and behave as if we are guilty even though we have truth on our side, because until at least one side does that, then both sides put up walls." He continues, people "are not going to go out of their way to come to our mosque. We have to come to them."

Sameya takes a similar and yet different take, "I've given my effort to give out an olive branch and if you've decided to deny it, that's okay." This takes a degree of responsibility to be the kind of person she wants to be, but this approach rejects the idea that she has to be the one responsible for changing other's minds and hearts.

In response to the question of what it is like to have people fear her, she says, "It's off setting at first. I've made the choice to try to make people comfortable who are around me, which I'm starting to not do lately. Lately I'm kind of like, either you fear me or you don't, either you're going to be comfortable or you're not. I'm not here on this earth to make you comfortable. Either you explore your fears and try to understand what you're scared of or get over it. We're living in 2018. We have all types of resources." In other words, if you are choosing to be ignorant and not explore it, that is not on Sameya. "I'm not here to make you comfortable."

Sameya talks about in the past how she would make herself "as small as possible. I would wave and smile at people, even though I'm introverted. I would force myself to be an extrovert just so people would be like, 'oh, she's safe, she's fine, she's not dangerous.'" It seems so strange to me that this lively, brilliant, beautiful, and endearing woman would have to work to prove to people that she's "not dangerous." It is a clear demonstration of "guilt by association." That kind of pressure is exactly what causes some people to become dangerous out of the removal of other options.

And the perceived danger, in Sameya's story, was clearly connected to markers identifying her with Islam. Almir Celebic (a kind, confident, encouraging, charismatic yet easy-going pharmacy student, young husband, former college soccer player, and first-generation immigrant from Bosnia) offers that his experience is different, given that he is "not prototypical." He continues, "Most people wouldn't recognize we're Muslim." Some of this is coming out of his community's experience of moving here from Bosnia, where it was not safe to be identified with any religion, so the practice of all religions had become more personalized, expressed more underground. Some of those practices carry over in their expression of Islam in the US as well. But this also accounts for the images that we have of "what a Muslim looks like." Almir's skin is lighter, his beard shorter. He can pass. But should he have to?

Rather than dispelling fear, for many, carrying the burden of diffusing other's fear causes renewed fear in the Muslim communities themselves. Sameya talks about taking her head scarf off as soon as her parents would drop her off at school when she was younger and how, "after 9/11, they [her parents] told me not to make any friends, because they thought everyone was dangerous." Sameya recounts that "even though I was hungry, even though I did want to play, I'd still say no," out of respect for her parents and the fear they had (and maybe have) for her.

Nairyna shares this fear for her kids, "for me, my biggest worry is when they go to school. Their name, their culture, their religion, their color—every single thing that makes them who they are is something they might get bullied about."

And the fear has added teeth because of how quickly things can go wrong. Arman talks about the stabbing that occurred on the Portland Trimet train in the summer of 2017. "I think it was thirteen seconds, he stabbed eleven times." And two were dead. "There's a change in how people express their dislike for Muslims. It's more physical, more vocal, more in your face."

This shifts our conversation to some of the specific experiences they have had, some of outright aggression, others of ignorance or even curiosity that came across wrong, as more harmful than supportive.

Nasreen starts things off, "I live in a condominium building right on the water front. It's a building where a lot of retired old people are. And they come up and see me in the elevator and always the comment is, 'aren't you hot? Isn't it too much?'" referring to her head covering. She continues, "they don't know, and they feel like they want me to feel comfortable. They think they are trying to help me but there isn't a good response to something like that. It's good intentions, I totally get it. It's not meant to feel comfortable as is. And I will not be more comfortable if I have less clothing on," she adds with a laugh.

Sahar offers one of her stories, "I think it was a couple of years back during Ramadan and I had stopped at a supermarket. And I was walking around the store with my head covering on and I was heading toward this cashier and this guy was following me from aisle to aisle. I could tell he's curious. He wants to say something. And I was trying to avoid him. And he found a quick opportunity to almost bump into me in one of the aisles and he just looked at me and he said, 'is it that cold that you have to cover yourself?' I looked at him and just smiled and didn't argue with him or anything but just walked away. But it shows ignorance. I mean, what does my scarf have to do with him? I understand it's the middle of the summer, it's hot, but the way he said it was almost like he wanted to get me to say something back to him. But I didn't say anything. I just smiled, giggled a little bit, and walked out, because I thought, if I say something in return, it's going to cause conflict and I don't want that."

Nairyna adds, "We definitely see people giving us dirty looks." She talks about a book fair that their mosque participated in where someone came up to her and called her a "traitor." She continues, "and a couple of weeks ago, we were driving and there was a car right next to us and they were giving us dirty stares. And it's scary because here they can have a concealed gun on them and can just shoot you."

Sameya tells a story of going to a restaurant with friends and visibly seeing others' nervousness, "everybody is scared, checking over their shoulders constantly, whispering, constantly looking at me. And then when you see more and more of us coming, you'll see people getting faster and faster done with their food. Then I think, how often will people be willing to make reservations for me if I'm going to empty out their business? Then as we're leaving, we'll see people who left earlier, just sitting around waiting as if they're going to save the restaurant if we're going to do something. Sometimes they'll follow us to our cars."

For grown adults to hang around and follow a group of teenagers and young adults to their cars borders on or crosses all the way into intimidation and inappropriate behavior. Many of us would be enraged if that happened to our children.

Sahar, thinking back to her story, says, "You have to be concerned about why they're concerned. And it's a little scary because, from my perspective, my heart was open to everybody around me and yet when he said that, all of a sudden, I went into this kind of fight or flight mode and I was like, I need to get out of this store. You get scared. You get nervous. Maybe he thought he was being funny, but it wasn't funny."

He could have been messing with her intentionally. He could have just been curious. He could have been making a joke. But impact is different from intentions.

Nasreen adds, "Especially in this day and age when Islam has become a global religion, when everybody knows Islam and a majority of people know that Muslim women do cover their heads if they choose to, whoever you see covering their heads, you can just respect the fact that they're covering. And you shouldn't be having any comments about whether or not they're hot or cold or whatever. It's our choice. Yes, it's 105 degrees and yes, I'm hot, but I don't need to hear it!" Everyone erupts into laughter.

Nasreen continues as the tone becomes more serious, "because, like we talk about, the jihad." Here Nasreen is talking about jihad as struggle. This goes beyond and is understood in Nasreen's community not as violence with the gun or sword but struggle against the things within our own lives that keep us from being our best selves for God. She continues, "The jihad against your own self, the demons that I'm fighting against me, nobody knows about them. You don't know what courage it takes for me to wear this piece of clothing on my head every morning and feel confident enough to walk through the door to face the world. So I don't need added aggression or added comments to wear me down. Because I'm a strong person, but someone else might not be. The teenage girls who are wearing hijab are facing so much hatred and insecurities and self-esteem issues and they are making the effort to do that because they feel it is the right thing to do. So we don't need added stress on them. They need to be free just like any other girl. This is the country where we are supposed to have the freedom of choice."

Sahar jumps in, "This is also about perception as well. 99 percent of Muslim women choose to do it because they think it's the right thing to do." Except in extreme circumstances, she assures, men are not forcing women to do anything. Women are making the choice. You do not have to understand why someone makes that choice to respect their right to do so. And in the case of Almir's mother, coming from a place where she was not allowed to wear her headscarf, now being able to choose to wear it feels good to her. It feels empowering to her. In some cases, the hijab = liberation, not the opposite.

Several of the stories are rooted in people simply not knowing what to say or do or what not to say or not to do. These Muslim neighbors I spoke with were incredibly generous and gracious about this, but also, it is exhausting and, for some, patience runs thin.

Arman speaks again about their community's emphasis on interfaith and public programs. He asserts that they understand that the media has different goals than they do "and we understand that people need to engage a real Muslim and ask questions." So they started a "Meet a Muslim: Ask Me Anything" campaign. This is the same campaign my friend Harris participates in that opened the chapter. Arman continues, often people don't know they have met a Muslim because of the environment. "People don't want to show that they are Muslim. You might be working with one, but you'd never know it." Fear factors in significantly here.

Arman tells of some of the experiences he, Harris, and others from their community have had by putting themselves out there in the public sphere. "We've had [other Muslims] tell us, 'thank you for what you're doing. I'd be too afraid to do it. God bless you.'" Fear is real.

Ignorance is, too, and Arman comments they are "trying to remove that as much as possible. We understand that the mosque might seem scary, but in public, you'll approach us, like at a mall or a coffee shop." Most of their experiences have been neutral or positive. Arman continues, "I would say 95 percent of people who come up to us will give us a high five, shake a hand, and the other 5 percent are curious and want to ask questions," but not for long. "I can count on one hand people who we've had 45–50 minute conversations with."

But there have been experiences that went sideways. Arman recounts times when "a guy was just kind of walking by and threw the F bomb" at them and an experience when someone came up and showed them a picture of the Malheur Nature Preserve occupiers from a couple of years ago and told them, "these guys are the real Americans" while engaging in a strange conversation only via typing. Arman also tells the story of "one lady who came with prepared questions to try to trap us. She had serious but misinformed questions about mistreating women, marrying underage, and all that. She rapid-fire asked them, didn't let me defend, and then was up and gone." Curiosity seemed to take a backseat to fear. "She had her mind set already."

Simply not accosting someone does not mean it is a positive experience, however. Arman shares deeper, "on a more intellectual level, I think people need to ask us questions, because I might was well be an ISIS recruiter, as far as they know." This demonstrates the pressure that our Muslim neighbors carry to not only prove themselves but also to fight against others who claim their same religion and do not hold ways of peace. They want a chance to educate us on what is good about Islam and to condemn how some people have co-opted it for different aims.

Arman continues, "But 95 percent don't [stop]. There is a problem. They should stop and ask questions and shouldn't just ignore everything that they hear. I wish people would stop by and ask us their questions." He tells the story of an encounter that models what he means, "one of my most memorable exchanges was with a sixteen year old girl from Seattle who was down with a volleyball team and she was asking some serious questions about women's rights and I think, since I wasn't giving her nonsense answers, it changed her mind a little bit. I wish the kind of questions she asked, others would ask."

The experiences of these particular people and their communities vary from mild to extreme, yet even the more mild experiences can cause harm.

Sameya talks about some of her experiences when people had good intentions, but missed. Sometimes people approach her to hear her story, but "sometimes there feels like an agenda." For example, "There's a class and they have to interview someone of a different faith. Every single time, I say no. Am I really the only person of a different faith on this campus? But it's harder to spot the person who is Jewish who lives right across from me." Sameya refuses to be a transaction in a larger agenda.

She also refuses to fit cleanly into identity boxes that people have. She says, "It's like I have to define what I am in fifteen minutes of us talking, you know? I'm Ethiopian. 'But aren't you Muslim?'" people will then ask. Sameya laughs at the absurdity of the question that she far too often gets. "Yes, I'm both." Having to define herself does not feel like love. Ignoring her identity also does not feel loving. Neither does not knowing anything about her or her community. And educating us is not always her job.

Part of this is in her own growth of sorting out what she is responsible for and what she is not. She tells about growing up post-9/11 and the burden she carried in school. "When we talk about situations like terrorist attacks and 9/11, people look at me like I have all the answers. Growing up, I took 100 percent blame for 9/11." Sameya was in kindergarten when it occurred. "When they said it's my fault, I took it! But after coming to [college], we sit down and think about these things. What is going on? Why do we have this stigma? What are we perpetuating? People do things out of fear so when they're scared they do things to make them feel safe. I'm trying to understand everybody else in America as to why they are scared of me and try to make them more comfortable," the latter of which she no longer feels the responsibility to do these days.

One example more on the extreme side of harm was, as Arman describes it, "a couple of years ago, we had some people show up at our mosque with some pretty bad signs and loud speakers."[13] He continues, "they were calling me pedophile and asked how many girls I had raped." He pauses, "I was coming for prayers and finding that at our doorstep."

If you watch the video on YouTube, you will see that the signs the aggressors held were proclaiming salvation from sin through Jesus. Which group is sinning here?

13. You can see a video of the incident here: https://www.youtube.com/watch?v=w1ZypJ1hINo.

Luckily, harm and indifference have not been the only experiences of our Muslim neighbors. I ask to hear stories of moments when people have been successful in providing care that really felt like care.

Almir speaks of the first day he arrived in the US at ten years old. They were able to come due to a relationship with his uncle who was already living here. But they were also welcomed by a church in Nashville, TN, who learned their story and paid for their first six months of rent and provided food, clothing, and other necessities to help them get started. "I don't know how else we would have been if they weren't there." This church's willingness to welcome Almir's family eased the shock of their immediate transition. That felt like love.

Nasreen and Sahar jump in with stories of friends showing up in important ways. "When I first got [to the US]," starts Nasreen, "at that time, Islam was basically nonexistent. Nobody knew what Islam was and what covering your head was. You didn't see anybody covering, so when I first started covering, I told my best friend, who is French, and she said 'I'll do it with you.' She was like, 'this is so Parisienne,'" Nasreen laughs, "and even though her legs were bare, she was saying, 'this is in support of you.' And she did that for me and throughout our school years, she did not take it off, even though she would want to."

She tells another example, "and my teachers respected me." She talked about one in particular, "The first time, I remember, he didn't know whether to bend down or shake my hand and it was so awkward, but he would learn." The experience was new, but her friends and professors put in effort to learn how to engage her with respect. They recognized that it meant something important to her. Almir similarly talks about professors who would make accommodations for his prayers.

Sahar tells one of her stories, "Some of my closest friends now are people who had many questions about Islam. A really good friend of mine here in America, she's Caucasian and she has not really travelled much outside of the US, she defends me and Islam more than I can probably defend Islam myself, just by living next door to me for so many years. She makes me so proud and literally teary eyed to think about it." Sahar continues, "She has sat in her family gatherings where some of her brothers-in-law have made fun of Islam or degraded Islam in some capacity and she has stood up and said, 'if you continue to talk this way, I'm going to leave this gathering.' That gives me hope. Knowing that she can do that for me, gives me hope."

Almir shares an example of a youth program at a church neighboring their mosque who has "always had a relationship with us." This small statement is key. This year, during Ramadan, the youth engaged in an activity and made a "giant poster with encouraging messages and then brought it over to us." This simple sign of recognizing another's religious holiday felt like love.

Almir also mentions the support of the police for their community, noting that the police chief has visited the mosque "and a couple of police officers have come and joined us for prayer." He shares that his community has not experienced overt hate in recent months, but they have noticed that their neighbors, sensitized to hateful language in the media today, have stepped up in a preventative kind of way.

Arman offers a practical example in a high pressure moment, "When 9/11 happened, there were flowers at the mosque all around the building that people had left as well as so many messages of support, along with hateful messages, on the voice machine. And when the 2016 election happened, people left flowers and messages at the mosque that they are with us."

Nairyna thinks back to one of the examples of harm listed above, "when the people were at the mosque yelling and cursing us, one lady was driving by and stopped and got out and was telling them not to do it, confronting them."

Arman adds, "I commend the lady that jumped out of her car to defend us. There are people willing to get into it. But we don't want people to take it to an extreme level where people are risking their lives" he continues, offering some other examples. "When 9/11 happened and even afterward, there were people who offered to get us groceries if we were too afraid to go out. Those actions are powerful and probably way more helpful than some others."

The actions range from the practical to the symbolic and sometimes both. Almir tells a story of his Bosnian community working to get July 11, a day that marks a painful day of much loss of life in the Bosnian Civil War, identified as a "Day of Remembrance for Bosnia where we acknowledge a genocide happening." He recounts achieving that designation and receiving a letter of support and offer of help from state officials as well as continued approvals to "march downtown and assemble when we want to mark that day."

Nasreen tells a story of receiving care from a different faith community. "We lived in a very Caucasian neighborhood in a very small town [a suburb of Chicago] and our mosque was in another area, so a majority of our community work was done where the mosque was. So me and my husband decided to do some interfaith dialogue in our area and we started a group in a church. They were very open and we started reading the Bible and the Holy Qur'an together as a part of an Abraham's children circle. That church basically took us in their open arms. They would talk about us in their Sunday services and come do work with us as well. And toward the end, we do a 'Muslims for Life' campaign as part of our denomination, so the first year they did it with our help. And every year subsequently after that, for almost eight years now, they've been holding that blood drive just to show support for us without any volunteers from our community. They set it up. They volunteer themselves. They put out the fliers as being our friends who are doing some work. That was so profound for me. It brought tears. And all of those people have shown support." She continues the story, reminding us of the discrimination their denomination also sometimes gets from other Muslims. "They also became friends with another sect. They invited them for an interfaith dialogue in Chicago at their church but when they asked them if they could invite us as friends, they refused and the whole community boycotted because they said, 'how can you talk about peace and love and an interfaith dialogue when you're excluding one portion of that community?'" So that communicated love, "that they stood up for us."

Sahar adds, "I think there needs to be honestly a lot more dialogue on a greater level, individually as well. If people just go beyond that fear and reach out to their local mosque, they'd be pleasantly surprised. Before they enter through the doors there's a completely different feeling and when they depart from the mosque nine out of ten are willing to come back and want to create more dialogue and talk more. And not necessarily even in religion, but show solidarity and be there as a part of humanity." She continues, "I remember when the Portland [Trimet] incident happened last year, I drove by a church that had posted something that said, 'Humanity for all. We welcome our Muslim brothers and sisters,' and I remember I actually stopped by and I took a bouquet of flowers just to say thanks. And I was so welcomed. They told me to take some cookies back home and they said, 'we'd love to start dialogue with your congregation. We'd love for you guys to come watch us when we pray and we would like to do that for you as well.' At the end of the day we all want the same things—happiness, love, to be respected, to be safe, acceptance from every culture and background. And the deeper you go to the core of who you are, it's pretty much the same thing."

Nasreen adds, "We can even get together on a social service basis, which we do a lot. If communities can get together in terms of social service, in terms of helping the community at large, I think that brings down barriers and brings communities together because you're working toward a bigger cause and people get to know each other fundamentally. We're made of the same things, even though the way of practicing religion may be different." This call to participate with our Muslim neighbors in community service and care was shared by several of the voices. It is also consistent with something that Eboo Patel and the Interfaith Youth Core affirm in their work, providing opportunities for people to work alongside one another toward a larger cause in making their shared neighborhoods better.

Nasreen continues with her story of the partner church, "We started doing food pantries together, doing one at the church and then at the mosque. We were all working together and we were more concerned about the people who were hungry. I think we need to focus on those things versus beating each other down about what we believe or don't believe. Just coming together as communities, because that's worth it. And I think that's what God wants us to do."

Sahar chimes in, "Absolutely and I think many different religious backgrounds do it on their own, but if two or three communities connected together, wouldn't that be such a powerful message to the rest of the world?" This sentiment is shared by the others.

Nasreen comments with another type of support, "I see these signs in a lot of shops, 'everyone is welcome.' Some even say something regarding hijab. That's a nice message to see because then you don't feel threatened."

Sahar sees it a little differently. "It's nice in a way but it's sad that you have to vocalize that. That's the reality of the times we're in. Never in all these years did I ever think that living in America we would have to see something like that and now almost every other store carries a sign like that. It kinds of pinches in a way. We accept you, but to some you're still the 'other.' That's the sad part about it. It pinches because of recognizing someone has to say it."

Nasreen picks up on this, "We are all the other to somebody. Why do we have to be?"

Sahar joins in, "If it's all fear based, you're not promoting love in any form."

Nasreen adds, "Love is accepting no matter who or what you are. Love doesn't categorize that you're perfect so I'm going to love you and if you're not perfect, I won't love you."

Sahar, building on this, says, "and we've seen examples of this in our own mosque, people who led completely different lives and by the grace of God are very different people today. Judgment has got to go."

Nasreen, finishing Sahar's thought, adds, "and how anyone gets to one point, we don't know what experiences they've gone through and what led to that behavior or those circumstances, how do you know? Who are we to judge them?"

Finishing each other's sentences now, Sahar states, "People change all the time. Life, dynamics, values, systems."

"You change for something you want to be. You grow. There's no growth if there's no change," Nasreen agrees. "We all have to become uncomfortable to be comfortable. So we need to get through this growing pain of talking to each other and being honest or we can never grow to where we want to be."

Sahar adds, "Things can't change until they change. Until you recognize there's a problem and face it, there's not going to be a change."

Nasreen tells a story demonstrating change, "We were raised in Pakistan, in terms of going out alone, you're not really going anywhere by yourself in Pakistan. So when I came here, everything was basically me. When I came to university, they would say, 'here's the subway,' and it was on me." She continues, "So, once I was taking a class in the evening from 6–9 so I took the subway and I was coming back and I realized that somebody had taken my wallet and all I had was, thank God, in my pocket, I had a subway token. So that's what I had to use to go home. So I was waiting for the subway for a train to come and I saw a big huge tall black man walking toward me. When I came to the states, a lot of people were telling me, 'you have to be aware of these kind of people. They can harm you, and this and that.' This person was coming toward me and I was wondering, is he going to harm me or why is he coming toward me? And thinking that, he comes up to me and he had a writing board and a paper, so he was raising money for something, and as soon as he asked me for money, I started crying. And I said, 'I don't have anything because my wallet has been stolen, and all I have is this token,' and I was telling him this whole story that my aunt would be worried, that I don't even have a quarter to call her and let her know that I'll be late because I missed my train. This poor soul, he looked at me and said, 'don't worry about it. It's absolutely fine and he pulls two quarters from his pocket and he gives me those quarters and was like, 'here. You can let your aunt know that you're okay and if you need anything, I'll be right here until the train comes and you don't have to worry about anything.' And that made me so solidified in my belief system that it's not about the color of your skin, it's all in your head, and if you really reach out to anybody, everybody could be your shelter. If you think with your heart, basically, it takes you to the right place."

The neighbors I talk to agree that many of the people they encounter have good intentions. Some care for them well. Others have missed. They also agree that the rhetoric about Muslims in the US sometimes emboldens people to do them harm. A few people want to do them harm. A few people provide great care. And a lot of people have good intentions but don't know what to say or don't know what to do. We have our own work to do in terms of understanding our implicit and explicit biases regarding Muslim people and the privileges afforded to Christian communities in the US. We have significant work to do in rooting out the factors that leave many of us frozen, not actively creating harm but also not actively diminishing it. I asked our neighbors for any additional advice they would offer to us.

Nairyna offers, "Clearly, the media isn't always telling the truth. Do a little research on your own and take the time to meet someone. In every religion, there's bad apples and people. One bad apple doesn't mean that everybody's like that." She is talking about both researching and discerning here. She also talks about fighting ignorance, "a lot of people don't even take the time to understand. They believe that 'Allah' means something else. No, it means God, like God in English, Dios in Spanish, Allah in Arabic. And I know my mom will always, *always* say whenever we hang up the phone, 'okay, pray to whatever God you believe in,' and I'm like, 'mom, I believe in God!'"

Arman affirms their similarities with others, "In interfaith, our goal is to show that we generally have the same type of issues in our lives as our neighbors. We have bills. We worry about our kids. We're not that alien to what could be considered the American experience, so if you take a moment to talk to us, for the vast majority of Muslims, you'll find us to be, you know, bearable," he says with a mix of seriousness and some tongue in cheek smirk recognizing the presence of the counter-messages about them.

He mentions a joke that he had seen, talking about "If a Muslim lives next to you," how "you won't have to worry about late night parties, alcohol, you know the kids will be going to school, etc." He emphasizes their normalcy.

Arman continues, "Just engaging in a conversation, it doesn't have to be about religion; for example, the last time we did a shelter visit, the youth that's responsible for that in our community invited one of his high school buddies with him. He showed up and helped us out. That's all I needed to see to see what kind of person he is. He sacrificed his time to do this work that he didn't have to do. If you engage in a conversation and have an experience together you can kind of see that, yeah, we follow a different religion, but we have the same issues, same concerns, same dreams. I have two kids and I want to make sure they're raised properly. 99 percent of us, we just want to make sure our kids grow up."

Arman also addresses some of the messages they hear about politically conservative US Americans. "Last year I was driving for [a rideshare company] a little bit and I picked up someone from a bar and he had a concealed carry in his pocket and voted for Trump but was super nice and said, 'If you respect me, I'll respect you, brother.' At the end of the day, the others too have the same concerns, same everything. We understand what they're going through and try to listen to them and explain, it's not the Mexican crossing the border to get the janitor job, it's the corporation trying to ship the job overseas. They feel like everything is being taken away from them. And on our side, I spent ten years in school to get the job I have. It wasn't handed to me. But it still feels like from your side of the perspective, you're losing things." There is a recognition of the need to know what life is like for one another to be able to work toward bigger goals out of shared values.

Nairyna continues the conversation, "A lot of people claim to know Islam and the bad things about it but if they actually take at least five minutes to open the Qur'an and just read it with an open mind and then make up your mind about what you think Islam is, that's a lot better than saying, 'all Muslims are fill in the blank.' And try to find someone who is trying to do good deeds as a Muslim." She tells about her godmother who is a devout Christian and who cares deeply for them. "She's completely Christian and he [Arman] is completely Muslim and we get along and we stay together and eat together. That relationship of interfaith is totally possible. She [her godmother] was confused at first and it started out awkward but she was open-minded. She wanted to know him because of respect for me."

It sounds like a no-brainer, but it is hard to care about people when we don't know them. When we get to know people, caring for them becomes much easier.

Almir reflects on this in his own life, saying, "I think it helps because I've had interests that I've pursued, extra curricular activities, and I think when you do stuff like that, you reach out to a different kind of community. That put me in places where I was just with other people and they got to know a little more of my personality and got to know me better." He continues, "The more comfortable you get with showing people who you are and what type of person you want to be and what type of life you want to have, that opens up more doors for people to understand how they can contribute to the relationship."

Sameya resists a little bit of the claims to sameness. She offers, "I always wanted to be like, 'I'm just the same as everyone else, but I'm not.' Talk to me like a normal person. Get to know who the person is first before you start to, like, categorize them. Come up to me with respect, dignity, humility, but without weird avoidance or pretending I'm not different." Somewhere between "She's not Muslim," ignoring that part of her identity in order to calm your own potential fears, and "She's only Muslim," reducing her to her faith. Sameya gives an example of a classmate at college who came up to her and said, "Hi, you're Sameya, right? And you're Muslim, right? I'm Jewish. Let's be friends."

Everyone emphasizes the need for us to do our own homework.

Nairyna suggests, "Do your research. Take the time to understand. Decipher if what you hear is right or wrong. Try to talk to someone in the community to decide for yourself if what you believe is right. And then, inform others around you. It's great if you learn yourself, but then spread out and take it further. And if that person has kids, they can raise them as better people."

Sameya echoes this, "You have to just get over the stereotypes and stigma that people tell you. Don't believe anything you hear, you have to go out and find it for yourself and then make your own judgment. Don't let things become 'fact' just because someone said it." And she asserts that a direct approach is a good one and that it is common in her community.

Love looks like direct, open, honest, conversation, not hiding. It also means that you do not rely on these neighbors to be your only teacher. Sameya asks that we do not ask her questions that we "could've googled."

She continues, "That doesn't feel like you want to get to know me. It feels like you're mocking me. They don't feel good to answer."

And what else feels like love cross-culturally and cross-religiously? Sameya chimes in, "Food is number one." Almir affirms this, talking about how even growing up, the cooks in his elementary school knew what foods he needed to avoid and always made him a little something they knew he would like to accommodate those needs. Perhaps the first areas of research could be to find out what our Muslim neighbors can or cannot eat as a part of their religious practice and then be prepared to share a meal together, as neighbors, with a chance to become friends.

A WAY FORWARD

In his TEDx talk,[14] Harris Zafar (the same Harris from the opening story), talks about our history of "othering" in the US and elsewhere. He refers to the WWII era Japanese incarceration/internment camps and the fact that being one-sixteenth Japanese descent was the only criteria needed to suspect you as a potential criminal at the time. He shows images of defamation and hatred of those with Japanese heritage to support these notions within the US psyche, creating Japanese people as the "enemy," the "other." This, as Harris says, "not only made them foreign to the American identity but also something to be feared and not trusted."

Harris refers to the African American experience also as "othering," and the dynamics of defining the normalized human experience as something polar opposite of African American people. He chronicles the history of forced conversions and forced expulsions of Jewish people, again with the propagandizing and dehumanizing images as support. The messages we hear and the images we view and make are formative for us. They directly correlate with how we perceive ourselves and others and, therefore, how we treat people. This is not always with rational intent, but sometimes they operate at the level of the subconscious.

Harris brings up these examples as a way to pose some profound and significant questions. "Why is it that seemingly good people," he asks, "good mothers and fathers, good neighbors and teachers, would allow and even join this vilification of others? How and why were humans able to not only demonize but persecute an entire population of people?" He offers

14. Zafar, "Demystifying the 'Other.'" See it here: *https://www.youtube.com/watch?v=rrgae7d6iI4.*

that at least one major reason, in his perspective, is the existence of mystery around them. These groups experiencing harm have been "categorically misunderstood by those victimizing them." Harris continues, "The simple act of not truly knowing about someone else or about others can be our greatest downfall." This not knowing leaves a blank space within our experiences and our discernment regarding the other. Then, when people are accused and vilified, we have a lack of knowledge to discern whether or not the accusations are true. We default to the images we have heard and seen. As Harris reminds us, "mistrust leads to fear." He continues, "Fear has driven humans to committing some of the most heinous acts imaginable throughout the course of history." Harris wrote his book, *Demystifying Islam,* to bridge the distance between Muslims and non-Muslims, to remove some of the mystery, to help create alarms inside us for when we hear accusations about the other that otherwise would not make sense. Bridging this distance is also why you will find him and Arman at the mall on Saturday afternoon with "Talk to a Muslim" t-shirts on and coffee and cake to share.

Bridging this distance does not have to be our Muslim neighbors' responsibility alone. In these conversations, we have heard many things that we can do to help meet them part way and, by doing so, show real love and support:

- We can do our own homework. Investigate what we do not know. Be discerning about what we believe about Muslim people. Identify what our questions and concerns are and then find someone to ask those questions to in a respectful and curious way.

- We can show up to learn more. If there is a mosque in our town or in a town nearby, call them and ask if there is a good time for visitors wanting to learn about Islam. Go to a mosque or an interfaith event hosted by the Muslim community in the area. Witness their prayers. Attend an educational or cultural event. Share food together. Or, if you live in a town without a mosque, find documentary films and stories positively and honestly demonstrating Muslim life.

- We can demonstrate concrete support. When an anti-Muslim event occurs anywhere, especially locally, put up a sign communicating that you care about your Muslim neighbors (see Sahar's and Almir's stories above). Call the local mosque and leave them a message of care and concern. Be mindful of food restrictions and plan accordingly. If you are a supervisor, make sure that your Muslim employees or students have the opportunity to pause for prayers. Offer to run errands for or accompany Muslim families if they are afraid to go out on their own. We can incur some of that risk ourselves.

- Actively re-humanize the Muslim community. This might need to happen in our own mind and heart, rooting out harmful untrue messages and reminding us of the sacredness of every person. It might also need to happen through speaking out to friends and neighbors if we hear speech that indicates otherwise. Commit to calling out hate speech whenever you hear it.

- Remember it is not our Muslim neighbor's job to make us feel comfortable. We can take ownership of and responsibility for our own discomfort and try to understand it. Take the role of guest with humility. Be a curious and respectful learner. Actively work to not make people uncomfortable for being who they are.

The words of Nasreen ring through my head as I write that last point. In her confident, yet gracious, and honest way, she says, "I'll be fifty in December and, excuse my language, I don't give a shit what people think of me." Among surprised laughs, she continues, "The only entity that I want to give a shit about me is God and if I'm pleasing him with whatever I'm doing, I don't care what people think of me. People around me know who I am and if somebody is going to judge me, let it be because I'm not answerable to them. I promised myself when I turn fifty, I'm not even going to think this much," she holds her first finger and thumb barely apart and continues, "about what people think. I need to be truly authentic to myself." Amen.

4

Home is Getting Toxic

Niceness, Having to Choose, and Being LGBTQ+ in the US Today

I HAVE NOT ANSWERED my phone for an unknown number in almost fifteen years. Yes, I come from a generation that prefers sending texts to making calls overall. However, that is not the main reason why I do not answer my phone. It has more to do with what happened the last time I picked up for a number I didn't know.

"[Name of the Organization], Leadership Development, this is Cassie," I said, running through the standard script of introduction in picking up the phone.

"How can you say that gay people are oppressed in this country?" the voice responded.

"Excuse me?" I stated, pretty sure that I had heard correctly, but buying myself a moment to take a deep breath to listen more to figure out the context of the statement (and giving my ears a chance to have been wrong).

"You write here in this thing that I got in the mail today that 'the God who delivered our ancestors from Egypt hears the cries of the poor and oppressed in our world.' And you list gay people in the list of these so-called poor and oppressed that we might find in our neighborhoods. How can you say that? How can a church-run publication print such a thing?" There was more than one accusation here.

He continued, "When they have so much of the wealth and power, how can you say that they are among the poor and oppressed, not to mention that God especially hears those people." This wasn't really a question. It was a statement dripping with contempt.

Every "they" and "those people," said with disgust, stung my ears. The sheer passion, completely unexpected when I had picked up the receiver merely a moment before, was like a cup of ice water thrust to the face . . . or a blistering flame. I physically winced.

I'm glad I don't remember who my caller was, but I will likely never forget the call itself.

There was a passion in the accusation that went beyond the question of whether or not the LGBTQ+ community should be included among those experiencing oppression. Rather, what my caller was stating was the idea that people who identify as LGBTQ+ cannot possibly warrant God's favor. This was a sentiment that I had heard before this conversation. When I included the LGBTQ+ community in my list, I knew what I was doing. I made the conscious decision to do it. I believed what I was writing, even if at the time I did not know what I believed about some of the pieces of the whole swirl surrounding it. I wrote it, submitted it, ran it through editing (where it passed with another set of eyes on it), printed it, and sent it out. When I received that call, I still believed it. When I hung up the phone, shaken, shivering from the coldness in the midst of the heat, stricken with grief and lament over what I had heard, I believed it just as much.

I also felt a new level of fear for any LGBTQ+ identifying person who might walk into a church with a leader like that. You can tell when someone doesn't want you there, even if they don't say it in words. It's hard to hear a message of grace when you know you're not wanted. My heart was broken. And I have not picked up my phone for an unknown number (even though I am at a different job in a different state across the country) in fifteen years.

THE FRAME

There is at least one major social issue that everyone recognizes is also a theological issue in each era. These have the power to split families, churches, and sometimes whole denominations. In our era right now, how we treat our LGBTQ+ neighbors is one of the biggest. At times, engaging this issue feels like a raging fire. At times, it feels like a storm that has already passed. And the landscape has clearly changed from where we once were.

Christian ethicist David Gushee, in *Changing Our Minds,* describes the shifts in perspective that have occurred in recent decades in the US regarding LGBTQ+ treatment and inclusion/exclusion. He discusses the fierce resistance from many Christian communities to the early "call for social equality" for LGBTQ+ people in the 1970s. He chronicles the ways that some faith communities saw discrimination against LGBTQ+ people in employment, adoption rights, housing, military and government service, and other industries as "a righteous crusade." He talks about the direct and indirect discrimination and bullying that occurred along with derogatory language on a regular basis against LGBTQ+ people, stemming sometimes from what people were hearing from the pulpit.[1] Clear condemnation seemed to be a key goal for many vocal groups, sometimes of particular behaviors, sometimes of people themselves.

This has not all disappeared. LGBTQ+ people continue to experience bullying and discrimination. They continue to receive harm from hetero-sexist and homophobic language and policies as we will explore briefly below. Yet, thankfully, as Gushee points out, many Christian communities now, regardless of their stance on sexual ethics, recognize the harmful effects of bullying in a general sense and that outright dehumanizing and degrading language toward any group of people is inappropriate and downright wrong.

As clinical and scientific understandings of human sexuality have changed, Gushee also notes that more and more Christians, even those who still hold to a traditionalist view of marriage, now accept that some people "simply are of same-sex orientation" and recognize that millions of people understand themselves to be LGBTQ+ "and that these core self-identities point to something real and significant that is counterproductive to ignore—even if the whole concept of sexual identity can be challenged as a modern construct."[2] This has not always been the case. It demonstrates a change in perspective.

And, as more and more of us get to know people who identify as LGBTQ+, our perspectives on what it means and what it means to engage our LGBTQ+ neighbors in Jesus-like ways are still changing. There remains a wide spectrum of approach to sexual ethics within faith communities. But Gushee suggests there are some baselines we can perhaps begin with—baselines that were not the same ones a few decades ago.

---

1. Gushee, *Changing Our Mind,* 30.
2. Ibid., 32.

Gushee continues:

> it is increasingly agreed, even on the traditionalist Christian side:
> gay people exist. It is wrong to call them names or use slurs about
> them. Their relationships should not be criminalized. They should
> not be discriminated against in employment, housing and public
> accommodation. They should not be bullied. They should never
> have to be afraid of violence as they go about their daily lives. They
> should not be blamed for America's security problems or social
> ills. They should not be stigmatized or treated with contempt.
> There should be no space in church life or culture for their dehu-
> manization and mistreatment.[3]

Gushee points out that these perspectives are held by most Christians
today, regardless of their stance on sexual ethics. And, he reminds us, if
we do agree with those statements, we "already support significant change
from what the Christian status quo was not long ago."[4] Our ideas about
LGBTQ+ inclusion are not the same today as they have been forever. That
does not necessarily mean we have already slipped down that proverbial
slippery slope. It may mean that we are getting closer to recognizing the full
humanity of our LGBTQ+ neighbors.

And still, we feel the embroilment and the pressures that come with
foundational questions about this component of current US American
Christian identity. "The culture war against sexual minorities began to
flourish in the early 1990s,"[5] says author Deborah Jian Lee. She continues,
"Very quickly, the widespread condemnation of gay people became integral
to the fabric of conservative Christian faith and its institutions."[6] Often,
this condemnation was articulated in terms such as "family values" and
came at a time as the message against divorce began to fall by the wayside.
Recognizing that divorce rates among Christian families were virtually
the same as everyone else's, many churches began to soften some of their
stances regarding divorce, performing marriages and ordaining clergy that
previously had been excluded. The new family values platform brought
condemnation of the LGBTQ+ community and their "lifestyle."[7] The fact
remains that this particular issue and this particular split has not always

---

3. Ibid.

4. Ibid., 33.

5. Lee, *Rescuing Jesus*, 69.

6. Ibid.

7. Ibid., 71.

been a dominant marker of Christianity, even conservative Christianity. And yet, we sometimes hear talk as though it is, and perhaps always has been, one of the most important issues of all of Christian theology and practice, sometimes even salvation.

It is clear that the heat continues to be turned on regarding the friction between those who are open and affirming toward our LGBTQ+ neighbors and those who believe that anything to do with LGBTQ+ living, identity, and culture is sinful and outside of God's will. In fact, the ways that we hear about anything pertaining to this issue sometimes overemphasize those poles as the only two choices. Perhaps even more troubling, this leads to harmful implications in our behavior toward one another, seen in the example of President Trump's inappropriate joking about the disturbing comment that Vice President Pence, heralded by many for his Christian faith, "wants to hang them all,"[8] in reference to the LGBTQ+ community.

So in the midst of these strong statements and polarizing policies that grow out of them, what is a faithful, responsible, Jesus-following person or community to do? What are we to think? The reality is that there are demarcated "Sides" in engaging our LGBTQ+ neighbors and the "LGBTQ+ issue." These are often categorized as Side A, Side B and Side X: Side A Christians "believe that God affirms same-sex relationships and marriage. In other words, same-sex behavior is not a sin."[9] Side B Christians "believe that having same-sex attraction is not inherently wrong, but that acting on it is sinful." Therefore, they suggest that LGBTQ+ Christians are "called by God to remain celibate."[10] And Side X Christians, "believe same-sex attraction *and* activity are sinful and that Jesus and therapy can reorient a person toward heterosexuality,"[11] notwithstanding that research has shown consistently that these therapies as a whole do not do what they set out to do and cause a great deal of harm in the process.[12]

It is important to note that these "Sides" also do not always fall cleanly along other dividing lines. And it is not uncommon for people to change

8. Brammer, "Trump Reportedly Jokes About Mike Pence."

9. Lee, *Rescuing Jesus,* 73.

10. Ibid.

11. Ibid.

12. See statements from the American Academy of Child and Adolescent Psychiatry, the American Academy of Pediatrics, American Association for Marriage and Family Therapy, American Counseling Association, American Medical Association, American Psychiatric Association, American School Counselor Association, National Association of Social Workers, and others at Human Rights Campaign, "Conversion Therapy."

sides throughout their life based on their experiences and seeking of truth and love. This has left faith communities with a few options regarding how they approach their LGBTQ+ neighbors (and sons and daughters and selves). Gushee has outlined these as:

- the "ask no questions" option,

- the "who are we to judge?" option,

- the "dialogue for discernment" option, and

- the "pastoral accommodation" option.

These options give responses that say, "We don't ask questions; we don't judge others; we are dialoguing about this, or consider this a disputable matter; we are doing pastoral accommodation to a church-full of broken people. Meanwhile, ya'll come, and we'll figure it out together with God's help."[13]

Others have taken what Gushee calls the "exclusionist" option, drawing the line for church membership, sometimes excluding any LGBTQ+ person, and more often, only welcoming LGBTQ+ people who choose to remain celibate. This raises complications, however, as Gushee explains, "because that 3.4 to 5 percent of the population is found in these congregations too." So, if "someone's child turns out to be gay," the congregation may have to "exile them from the Church unless they commit to celibacy."[14] Often this leads to closeted people who feel unsafe within the faith community that raised them.

That leaves one more option, according to Gushee: The "normative reconsideration" option. "Some churches have studied the biblical texts and Christian tradition and contemporary realities and arrived at the conclusion that the heterosexual-only ethic needs to be revised."[15] Almost never does this mean that all parameters of sexual ethics are thrown out the window. Rather, it often means that for these churches, there is simply not enough biblical evidence to suggest that what exists as committed same-sex relationships and/or LGBTQ+ identity today is what was being critiqued or condemned in the oft-quoted biblical passages. For these churches and Christians, there is a recognition that our context is different than the context of the biblical writers and they conclude that the evidence suggests

13. Gushee, *Changing Our Mind*, 41.

14. Ibid., 42.

15. Ibid., 43.

that what they are talking about and what we are asking about are likely not the same things.[16] In fact, the differences between then and now may be as vast as those on opposite sides of the current "Culture Wars" on this issue feel. For these churches and Christians, the typically quoted passages need to be rethought in light of other biblical messages, with a deeper dive into both the original context as well as our own, and with this, the markers of healthy relationships may need to be re-engaged for same-sex and heterosexual couples alike. This is not a disrespecting of the biblical text as authoritative, but a re-centering of other components of the gospel as the lens through which to read and discern the heart of God on this and other matters.

The Heart of the Matter

In his paper, *Love is the Great Endeavor,* Irish theologian and poet, Pádraig Ó Tuama, reflects on an experience, while working as a chaplain, of having someone ask him "Why are you a Christian?" Ó Tuama runs through a few reasons he could offer in response to this question and then states:

> In the event, I told the person who asked me why I'm a Christian that I'm a Christian because I love Jesus. I have been excluded from Christian organisations, intimidated from streets where I lived, un-invited from friendship and professional circles and made to feel ignorable because as a gay man, my words were deemed to be automatically dismissible. But I have never felt that the Gospel treated me that way.[17]

He continues, "In the gospel, I hear the voices of all kinds of people trying to figure out what it means to be human."[18] And this question of "human-ness," and what it means has been both flaunted and defined to the exclusion of many throughout our history, as we have already begun to see in previous chapters. The LGBTQ+ community is included in that number. Ó Tuama asserts this poignantly in recounting, "The question on

16. There are several books that explore the biblical passages in particular. If you are interested in digging deeper into that conversation, especially to understand how scholars and faith communities read the passages in a way that does not automatically support a traditionalist view, but that handles the text with respect, consider Gushee, *Changing Our Mind.*

17. Ó Tuama, *Love is the Great Endeavor,* 2.

18. Ibid.

our school playground was whether you were homosexual or homosapien. I learnt early that you had to remember the answer that wasn't going to get you beaten up."[19]

LGBTQ+ inclusion or exclusion is both a theological and political issue for many in our time and place. However, it is both, neither, and more than that for most people in my generation and those younger than us. That includes both those who identify as LGBTQ+ and those who do not. For us, this is primarily a relational issue. It is an existential issue. "It's a question of how much space and grace we will make for friends we dearly love, and friends whose differences have made them feel incredibly alone, afraid and unloved."[20] To us, this is a love issue and not only what kind of love is and will be sanctioned by the church for marriage, but also how the church will care for or dismiss people who identify as LGBTQ+ and who we deeply love. There are significant implications for these responses, both for the church and our LGBTQ+ neighbors.

It is no secret that mental health in the LGBTQ+ community, especially among young people, is a cause for concern. Yolanda Turner, professor of psychology at Eastern University, and who specializes in the intersections of faith and sexuality, comments in an interview with Deborah Jian Lee that, "It's hard enough for kids who are in their twenties who have been taught that they're full of sin to love themselves anyway . . . But to also hear that the core of who you are is unacceptable to God is really shaming, and so the internalized loathing is compounded by the fact that God thinks that too. It's a whole other layer of psychological injury."[21]

Recently, I was asked by a student group on our campus to help them put together a panel of people in our city who identify as LGBTQ+ and who are leaders in their faith communities to talk about how they reconcile those two components of their identities. In listening to some of my friends on that panel of Jewish, Buddhist, and Christian faith leaders, I was struck again with the pain that many of them have experienced in the struggle to be able to be a faithful version of themselves in the world. I was especially struck when two of my friends, Isaac and Joshua, told their stories of growing up in Christian families and Christian faith communities. Both professed that as they came to realize their own sexual identity, their experience was one of anguish knowing that in their faith communities they

19. Ibid., 1.

20. Matthew Vines in his introduction to Gushee, *Changing Our Mind,* xxv.

21. Lee, *Rescuing Jesus,* 76.

could not be both gay and Christian. Two components that were key in their identity in the world were in conflict and, in Joshua's story, his reality was further compounded by race.

It is a miracle that both Isaac and Joshua lived to sit on that panel that day. Both told their stories of suicide attempts. They told their stories of praying for relief, praying to be changed, of being sent to reparative therapy to reverse their sexual identity. One even married a woman because he thought for sure that God would use that experience to "heal him." It didn't. These experiences caused both to leave Christianity. Their stories were such a contrast to my friend Deborah, who was not made to feel that her sexual identity was a "deal-breaker" for life or wholeness in her communities. Joshua left for a Buddhist community who welcomed him whole. Isaac reconsidered Christianity only after being befriended by a Christian pastor who had been kicked out of his denomination for affirming LGBTQ+ people. Both Isaac and Joshua are now brilliant leaders in their faith communities because of that connection with people who received them as they are. They sat there telling their stories that night as two men who had come to accept themselves, their whole selves, and as two men who had found faith communities who embraced them and who now were benefitting from their thoughtful and compassionate gifts. The stories of process, of being accompanied and not left alone, of finding a place within a community and within oneself to live into and through these foundational questions was music to my hurting students' ears. For this story of rejection is far too common. And it is oh, so damaging and dangerous.

Youth identifying as lesbian, gay, or bisexual are "four times more likely to attempt suicide" than their non-LGBTQ+ peers.[22] The statistics among transgender people are just, if not more, alarming, with "57 percent of those who face family rejection attempting suicide and over 50 percent of those who face discrimination at school attempting suicide."[23] Faith communities are complicit in the self-hatred of our LGBTQ+ neighbors and youth. "[T]oday's queer Christians face alarming mental health risks, especially *because* of their nonaffirming Christian communities."[24] The loss of life is serious. Period. And as Amelia Markham, a queer Christian activist, states, "There are some serious questions we have to begin asking ourselves if maintaining one interpretation of our sacred text is demonstra-

22. Kann et al., "Sexuality Identity," 14, in Lee, *Rescuing Jesus*, 75.

23. Haas, et al., "Suicide Attempts," in Lee, *Rescuing Jesus*, 75.

24. Lee, *Rescuing Jesus*, 75.

bly linked to bodily harm and spiritual devastation for an entire group of people."[25] Refusing to listen to those questions is not love. We are at least partially at fault. It would do us well to consider the responsibility of this complicity as there is simply no excuse for churches to not be safe places for people of all kinds.

In fact, the stories and data suggest that simply the removal of rejection can increase someone's mental health and self-perception. Lee reports that "According to a 2012 study, twelve months after Massachusetts legalized gay marriage, medical and mental health care visits among gay men sharply declined."[26] Two of the main factors toward positive mental-health and self-perception are the ability to be honest with oneself and the people around you about who you love and having that identity received in a way that does not automatically condemn it. These simple and profound experiences can bring a significant degree of healing.[27] This might sound fairly obvious when we read it and certainly might to those who have heard or been a part of heartbreaking stories of rejection and learned self-hatred. However, if you have not experienced this kind of rejection or have not watched as someone you love experiences this kind of rejection, it may simply never (have had to) cross your mind. That does not mean that our actions do not still directly impact the kind of environment and policies that we have for those who are affected.

When we vote for exclusion (whether intentionally or because we simply never thought about the impacts on gender and sexual minorities), there are repercussions beyond law and policy. The statistics of self-harm for LGBTQ+ people are only one indication of that. Research has shown that even if we cannot be fully affirming, simply a refusal to reject has impact on mental health. So, even if our theology is not in a place where we can advocate for full inclusion of our LGBTQ+ neighbors in all aspects, simply choosing to not reject another human being makes a real, concrete, potentially immediate difference. This is an arena where all of us can contribute. And it needs to be a true non-rejection, not a more quiet rejection.

When we choose to not reject, we can make room to begin to legitimately get to know people and, out of that knowing, offer love. According to the Human Rights Campaign's "Coming Out Day's Youth Report," clergy

25. Qtd. in Kuruvilla, "Link Between Religion and Suicide."

26. Hatzenbuehler et al., "Effects of Same-Sex Marriage Laws," in Lee, *Rescuing Jesus*, 77.

27. Lee, *Rescuing Jesus*, 77.

and one's religious community were the communities that LGBTQ+ youth were least likely to come out to.[28] Least likely. How can we care for people if they are unable to be themselves or be honest about who they are to us? And can someone feel loved if they cannot feel safe to tell us the truth about their lives?

This is a question of what does good news sound like to those who quite honestly could use some right now. It is a question of what does it look or sound like to love those who have been told that the ways they feel and express love are at best suspect or at worst an abomination to God. This goes much deeper than correct theology or partisan politics. And it is, very simply and most definitely, at least one of the issues that will define the church of the twenty-first century. For many in my generation and younger, it often is the deal-breaker of our ability or inability to be a part of a church community anymore. The stakes are high. We need some help.

THE CONVERSATIONS

Recognizing this, I spent some time over the past several months listening to the stories of friends and students who identify as LGBTQ+ asking them what looks, sounds, and feels like love right now and what doesn't. I heard stories of coming out that went well and those that went painfully wrong. I heard stories of faith communities that were welcoming and those that were unsure but stuck with the process and the relationship with the person. I heard stories of those who slowly cut ties with their LGBTQ+ child/neighbor/sibling/friend without fanfare and those whose separation was loud and violent. I often heard of communities that simply gave off the vibe of unwelcoming, while not saying it outright, leaving people to wrestle in fear and isolation and uncertainty. For many, their religious identity has been significant in shaping the process.

One loveable college student, Alaine Morgan ("an arts kid," known for her dry wit, her deep honest compassion, and her ability with thoughtful words to speak directly to the core of a moment), echoes Isaac's and Joshua's experience above when she says, "I remember the religion portion being huge for me when I first was figuring everything out, because I never saw it as you can have both. It was always 'you can have this [being Christian] or you can have that [being gay].' When I first started realizing that, 'oh crap,

28. Human Rights Campaign, "Coming Out Day's Youth Report."

I'm queer,' it was like, 'I guess I can't have this [Christianity] anymore. That was a huge tug of war for me."

John Hamilton, (a lanky, understated, and endearingly quirky college athlete from a small town now navigating city life, loved by his peers and staff alike) jumps in, "It's part of your culture, too. It's a part of me, so it's hard to throw all of that away. And at the same time, I'd be okay to never go back to that church again," referring to the church he grew up in. That is a strong statement. It is a statement that carries grief and also a sense of resolve and lack of hope that the community that raised him could be a place that cares for him now. There is an indictment and a wish in that statement.

In talking with Kori DeSimone (a vibrant poet and social service worker, known for her heartfelt advocacy and care, and whose heart beats for equity and justice in the world), she tells me a story that started rough, but turned redemptive in a hurry. It was the story of Kori coming out to her "very best friend in the whole world," Mollie. Kori describes how she caught Mollie off guard after a long night of studying and Taco Bell in college and, Kori says, "I told her that I thought I was identifying as Bi. And she stared at me and said, 'Why?'"

This is a pattern in some of the stories that I heard. How the hearer responds in a crucial moment like coming out has significant impact not only on the person coming out but also on the relationship between the two. This is not unique to coming out stories. It is true about all of our responses in any moment that takes such courage. And coming out takes courage.

Sarah Kudrna (a bubbly and energetic student and barista with a depth that is apparent directly below the surface and a humor that shows readily in her cross-stitching patterns) tells the story of coming out to her little sister. "I came out to my sister because I was bringing [Sarah's partner] to my best friend's wedding. I brought her into my room and I sat her down and I said, 'hey, I'm bringing a date to the wedding. And my sister said, 'I know, I heard you talking to mom.' And I said, 'well, this person is a girl. You've met her. She's come over here before. We're dating.' And she just sat there and she nodded. And I said, 'so what do you think about that?' I had come out to my parents a couple of weeks before and my sister was the last person I came out to. And my sister looked at me dead in the eyes and said, 'I love you, but I will never approve of this and this will never be okay with me.'"

Sarah continues, holding back tears, "My sister is eighteen, she is my best friend in the whole world and at her core, she is kind, loving, and funnier than almost anyone I know. I said to her, 'Let's talk about this, I'm a religion major, I know that the reason you're not okay is because of religion.' Sarah pauses before continuing, "And she said, 'It'll never be okay with me. No matter what you say, you'll never change my mind.' So to hear my favorite person in the world say to me, 'I will never be okay with you being happy and I will never be okay with you being loved and with you loving yourself,' basically, that's what it felt like. I have had to look at some of the people I love the most in the world, including my little sister, and realize that they have a lot of homophobia. Homophobia that I recognized in myself at the beginning of my coming out process and continue to see pop up now. Homophobia that I continue to fight but my family doesn't seem too keen to change, not totally realizing that it affects me in my daily life living at home. Home has become really toxic." [See more about Sarah at www.loveinatimeoffear.com and click on the video of Sarah.]

Responses like this are why people like John and Alaine have not come out to their families. They are not alone. And it does not always go like this—back to Kori and Mollie.

In telling the story, Kori admits that she does not remember the next few minutes in very clear detail. She remembers stumbling through some kind of canned responses to Mollie while also trying to figure out how to process Mollie's reaction. However, as Kori tells it, the next day made all the difference.

"The next day," Kori recounts, "She had written on a notecard that said on one side 'why are you bi'—she owned the words she used—and then on the other side she wrote 'because you are strong and because you are you and you are being authentic and you are falling in love.' It felt like love," Kori said, "for her to realize she messed up, owned it, thought about it, and did her homework." And then Mollie took another step.

Kori continues, "Mollie was the student chaplain the year I came out and she knew I felt comfortable praying for people in more public settings." It was a practice for a couple of students to be available as prayer partners during school chapel services for those who might want it. Mollie continued to ask Kori to serve in this role after Kori came out to her.

Kori talks through the impact of that action. "I was so nervous and I remember standing up there panicking inside and I remember saying to God, 'is this right? Am I okay? Am I missing something? Did I make a mistake?' All of these voices and questions. People would come to me for prayer and I kept thinking, 'am I a liar? Am I wrong? Should I have this position?' And I felt like God saying, 'I love you and I put you here and people are coming because they feel comfortable and safe and you're exactly where you're supposed to be.' And I remember being thankful and people still kept coming and still kept coming. And that felt like love that I could be in that space that during my childhood did not feel open or helpful with that part of me and knowing that I could be real with myself and pray for people and talk to God and not be hiding."

Mollie gave the gift to Kori of saying—you don't have to hide. And this news about you is not going to be the deal-breaker regarding everything else I have known and seen of you. Mollie chose to go with the good fruits she had seen of Kori's care for the community over and against Kori's sexual identity as the decision making factor. That felt like a knowing, concrete, and much needed love to Kori in a moment when she had a lot of fears and concerns.

That experience was especially meaningful because it was not the only response that Kori got. She talks about some of these other experiences, her unique brand of completely sincere sassiness leaking through. "There were multiple people who reached out to me saying 'I'm praying for you, I hope you realize the truth of the abuse of your childhood because this is obviously where this is coming from. I hope you remember God's word.' And that just cropped up because I was in a relationship with a woman. They weren't around when I needed that in prior parts of my life. When I really felt like I was not close to God, they didn't show up. When I was with a man and it was destructive and abusive, they didn't see it as harmful. But as soon as I was in a healthy, loving, committed relationship with a woman, God needed to be hearing what was going on and they wanted to make sure that I knew that they were in communication with God over my life and that I should get back into communication. That was painful."

These comments in this moment did not feel like love to Kori. It felt more like judgment. The concern felt less for Kori's well-being and more like an opportunity to express a sense of one's own "rightness" in the face of Kori's "wrongness." That kind of mixing of Christianity with rejection or selective concern is one thing that makes it so hard for people like Kori, Alaine, and John to trust the church or people associated with it.

Many of the people who reached out to Kori in that way were family members. Kori and her partner, Shayla Collier (the quieter of the two whose laugh lights up a room, who I go to to talk basketball, and who carries a unique balance of both steadiness and effervescence) talk about the difficulties of family dynamics. Shayla tells a story about being asked by her boss how her "sister" was doing, refusing to recognize her relationship with Kori, even when corrected. When they told the story to Kori's parents, they remember the discomfort Kori's parents showed in hearing it. They reminded Kori and Shayla that their boss, who was also Kori's parents' neighbor, would "bring over treats" and do other "nice" things. In their minds, there seemed to be a conflict between thinking of someone as "nice" and also being able to recognize the harm that they might be causing to others with homophobic behavior. They are not alone in this.

Kori and Shayla recognize the tension that can cause, but ask for a reframing. "What would it look like," Kori begins, "for them to not say 'oh, but he's a nice guy,' but to say 'oh, he's done these nice things and he's said these hurtful things'?" This reframing makes room for Kori and Shayla to be heard and believed rather than immediately made invisible again. They repeat many times that they are not asking for a total overhaul all at once, but some simple steps forward. "Let yourself be vulnerable enough to be curious about how 'niceness' and actions that cause harm can happen at the same time in the same person," Kori adds.

Shayla continues, "if they can't understand by just us telling them what happened, it would be helpful for them to ask, 'how did you feel? Why did you feel that?' Ask questions rather than just brushing it off because they feel uncomfortable." The main point here is: if you don't understand, try to. Listen. Let the impacted person be the one to tell their own story and decide what kinds of next steps might occur. Hear their reading of it before you offer yours (if you offer yours at all in that moment).

Shayla picks up on that further, "It's almost like everyone listens assuming that we want them to do something for us or handle it for us but we don't want that. We want support, but we can also handle ourselves. We don't need them to be our voice." We recognize together that the dynamics can be especially tricky when it is your parents or another person who is supposed to protect or care for you, if it is someone that has had the impulse in the past to fix things and, especially, if that person is unsure about the LGBTQ+ community. But this isn't something Shayla and Kori always want fixed. They want heard. There's a fine and important line between protection and empowerment sometimes. And it takes really knowing and loving a person to be able to discern which it is that they need from you in any particular moment.

Kori's story illustrates this a bit further as she talks about coming out to her mom. When she told her, her mom cried, "because she said that she'd been an advocate for me in my whole life and 'for this one thing I can't protect you.'" Kori continues, "I think when my parents don't know how to handle and when they choose to normalize, I think it's because they think if they normalize, I won't feel pain."

Kori tells a story of being at a restaurant as a family and noticing that a woman at a different table was giving Shayla and her a look of disgust. Her family did not seem to notice. Sometimes she feels the "not noticing" is a choosing not to notice. "I'm not asking them to look but I'm asking them to recognize that we may share the same room but we don't share the same space and it doesn't mean the same thing. And if they just recognize that, it feels different."

Others also echo this, saying that it feels like love when people recognize that much of the world is not set up for them and that they have to fight constantly to simply exist and belong. That recognition comes across as love or at least a pathway to concrete love because it allows our LGBTQ+ neighbors to be seen and it is a choosing to realize that their lives are different in some important ways. It also is a way of continuing to say that for our lives to change because theirs are different is not an inconvenience but an act of love.

To show concrete love to our LGBTQ+ neighbors and friends is to be willing to enter into uncomfortable spaces. They know what that feels like daily. Kori and Shayla's advice: Don't shut down a conversation because you're uncomfortable. Ask questions. If you don't understand, admit it. Get curious. Try to understand. Calm down your hero complex and let them have control of their own story. Sometimes they don't need us to rescue them. They need us to show up and show support in different kinds of ways.

Sarah tells a story that reflects some of this in a small step. She tells the story of going out with her parents and some of their church friends for her dad's birthday. She brought her girlfriend with her. She reflects on the experience saying, "none of them said anything and they talked to us and they talked to me as they always have and they talked to [her partner] like they normally would. And it was like, I don't know if these people are affirming or not but just the simple fact that no one was a dick was amazing."

Sarah continues, still laughing about her word choice in her last statement, "My mom has been very open about the fact that she is not very comfortable using the term girlfriend. She says, 'she's your _____ [using Sarah's partner's name],' but when she introduces us to other people she introduces her as my girlfriend because she knows that that's what she is to me. Even if she's not comfortable with it, she is taking the step that says, 'I know who this person is to you and even if I'm not comfortable with it, I will respect the fact that this is this person to you' and that has been an act of love from people who aren't affirming people. Even if you don't like it, you accept that this person is who they are."

Kori gives some simple suggestions: "I'm thinking long-term, if there's a person who is reading this or listening and wants to turn their ears off because of shame for handling things in unhelpful ways in the past and dealing with shame is difficult, if you're faced with those moments, if you can just say, 'I'm sorry, that sounds hard.' If you feel like as a human to human you can handle that, you don't always need to say anything else. But maybe when you're by yourself ask yourself why you're uncomfortable and what's making you uncomfortable. If you feel like you're compromising something or if you have conflicting voices in your head or you feel like you're expected to do something, do the long work by yourself. And start with 'I hear you.' That's what I want. I don't need everyone to come and be my champion or my corrector. I would love this to be a little bit better by everyone doing their own work themselves."

Sarah echoes these suggestions, "Trust people and allow people to be experts on themselves. Although something may be new to you, this is not new. This is something that a lot of us think about and we process over for months or years. Just trust people. And my second piece of advice is to ask questions. If you can't ask questions to the person, because sometimes when people first come out, they can't have those conversations, find someone to talk to because people in the LGBTQ community are willing to answer those questions even if they're really shitty questions. They may not be the person who came out to you but there's someone out there who is willing and who has already answered those questions and is there to talk to you. And please, dear God, talk to them. Don't talk to a straight ally. Don't talk to someone in a non-affirming church. Find someone who is in the LGBTQ+ community and talk to them and learn from the source the things you need to know."

Be curious. Show interest. Ask questions. Attempt a relationship. Risk admitting what you do not know. Keep trying to know. These are echoed over and over.

John states, "get to know someone who is gay or LGBT. I had two different old guys from my town who said, 'you really changed how I thought about gay people' because they didn't know anyone before me." Simply knowing someone who identifies as LGBTQ+ has been a significant part of the reframing of the conversation and policies over the past decade. A lot of it, in John's opinion, has to do with "Seeing that gay people really aren't that different."

Alaine gives her affirmation as well, with a dose of sarcasm along with it, "also, God forbid you do a little research for yourself. Google is free. And you can take two seconds to figure out what queer and transgender and bisexual and all that means."

Shayla adds, "I'm willing to answer any sort of questions people have but I'm not willing to baby somebody because they feel uncomfortable. I'm not willing to have to teach them 24/7."

And Beth Kosmowski (fun-loving and loyal, known for her scientific brain, goofy puns, and a ready smile that immediately removes any doubt as to whether or not you belong) asserts, if you do disagree, "just don't express it negatively." What people need in those moments is not your judgment but your presence. Ask, "would you like to tell me more?" Ask "what do you think are next steps for you?" Ask, "how can I care for or support you right now?" Maybe even ask and be willing to hear and learn how they reconcile their sexuality with their faith. For many those two have been in conflict and for many others they work together in life-giving ways.

Sarah shares how sexuality and faith "were at war" for most of her life because of her religious context. But in her process of seeking the heart of God and trying to learn to love herself, things changed. "I have come to a place where I believe that at the core God is love and when love is real and love is healthy, that means that God is there." She continues, "My sexuality has allowed me to fall in love with myself and look in the mirror and like what I see. It has allowed me to find that love that the Bible talks about."

Offering love can be complex or really simple. The ways of harm have also been.

"There have definitely been some really big things," says John, "but I feel like the most are just a bunch of little things, just like growing up constantly with 'oh, you have a friend that's a girl, why aren't you dating her?' and 'you should do this, you're a guy.' A lot of 'you shouldn't do this kind of thing' are the things that have scarred the most because they happen so often."

Or, as Sarah adds, "it doesn't feel like love when someone says they 'still' love you." It reminds them that this factor of their identity could be and often is a deal-breaker.

Then there are those that do not seem so small, like likening being LGBTQ+ with addiction. Beth tells a story from her own experience. "I think what really hurt me in these past few months is that, I came out to larger family by letters and one of the responses back to my mom was 'well, if Bethany was doing drugs, you would intervene,' so to compare this to me doing something harmful to my body, to categorize it like that, it's something totally different. So even if you disagree, don't compare it to something as damaging as taking drugs."

Alaine gives another harmful example. "I was going to a little Christian school that was super, super strict and had a set in stone defined code of ethics and literally you opened up the handbook and homosexuality was defined in like a paragraph long sentence of things you couldn't do along with rape and incest." She continues, "I thought I could handle it because I grew up with this and I've been dealing with this forever and I was like, 'okay, I'm used to this. I can handle another four years.' Then I got there and it was such a hard juxtaposition because there was so much good Christian love and so much religion. I felt so connected and plugged into God. And at the same time we had daily chapel and sometimes they would have really homophobic speakers and you look around and you see people agreeing with that and by the middle of my first semester I was already looking for a new school."

It is not uncommon for faith communities to identify homosexuality as "like any other sin." In one sense, this makes it not an extra big deal. In another sense, however, it is a big deal for our LGBTQ+ neighbors and that categorization continues to communicate messages about personhood that cut to the core of LGBTQ+ people. In these instances, it likens what they experience as life-giving expressions of love to the same category as violent crimes. In order to feel like love, our LGBTQ+ neighbors ask that the conversation shift toward a wider understanding of healthy relationships (beyond the biological sex of the partners alone) and, informed by that, then come back to the conversation about sin and goodness.

It is also not uncommon to diminish the weightiness of LGBTQ+ relationships. Shayla tells about complicated dynamics with a family member who she deeply loves who was posting "hateful things with the bathroom ban or transgender people in general or marriage equality things." She remembers, "At one point I finally commented that this is very hurtful. He said something about 'why is marriage important to you? It's just a piece of paper.' That comment is never said to heterosexual couples. It's so much more than a piece of paper. If Kori was in the hospital, I'd be able to make decisions. We would have health care or custody of our babies. All of these things come with a piece of paper." Those comments have consequences. Shayla continues, "I haven't talked to him for a year and a half now because of that conversation."

Sometimes harm comes in direct ways. Sometimes it comes in minimizing. Sometimes it comes by simply not realizing the differences in very practical experiences between LGBTQ+ people and heterosexual people. Not knowing does not make it less harmful.

And, although harm abounds, harm is not the whole of the experience. Alaine transferred to another college across the country. Her new school is also affiliated with the Christian faith and is still navigating what it means to reckon with historic understandings of that while genuinely caring for LGBTQ+ students. This continues to be complicated at times. Alaine tells a story about someone saying something inappropriate to her at her new school, but her experience was met with a different kind of reaction. Having heard this, the next day her RA and a staff member, Serena Cline, contacted her and let her know, "if you don't feel safe and if you need someone to step in here, we're 100% on your side. We'll treat this just like we'd treat a racial injustice on this campus. We want you to know we are behind you and here are some options that you have." Alaine continues, "in that moment of knowing that I was seen and that this wasn't ignored and that there are people on campus that are behind me, I felt really loved."

A WAY FORWARD

Things are complicated. Many faith communities feel a significant tension between a traditionalist sexual ethic and a desire to show real care to our LGBTQ+ neighbors. There are significant tensions, even contradictions, between traditionalist readings of the oft-quoted scripture passages and the ability to show the kind of care that our LGBTQ+ neighbors need, deserve, and are asking for. In order to show real love, deep, honest reflection in relationships with LGBTQ+ people has to be part of the equation. This includes listening to their voices and not simply making our decisions and then talking at them. We need to quit saying in our arguments that this "isn't personal." It is deeply personal. If it doesn't feel personal to us, perhaps we need to make it personal to our lives and quit deflecting the fact that it is very personal to the lives of our LGBTQ+ neighbors.

Even so, perhaps some things do not have to be as complicated as the barriers we have constructed seem to make them to be. From these brilliant LGBTQ+ identifying people, I heard that they are tired of hearing about a "gay agenda" or "lifestyle," which seems largely built out of assumptions that cloud the truth and cause more rejection. As Ó Tuama asserts:

> Here's the gay agenda.
>
> - Survive the day, and love.
> - Survive the day without being beaten up, or fired, or told to be quiet about promoting your sexuality when all you're doing is talking about your holiday.
> - Survive the day when somebody says "how can you reach out to your gay neighbour with the gospel?" indicating that often people think it's impossible for your gay neighbour to already love the gospel.
> - Survive the organisation that says "if we have to be kind to you, then that's us being oppressed"
> - Survive the voice that says "What you call love, isn't love"
> - Survive the public voice on radio that says "We'll use our words for you, not your words for you"
> - Survive the voice that says "we'll define you by what we imagine you do in bed with all those lots of people we imagine you sleep with."
> - Be generous.
> - Try to believe it when people say they don't mean it personally, even though it's all personal.
> - Recognise that even when people say your love with your partner is as a result of being abused that somehow, it's possible to still speak cordially to each other.
>
> THIS is the gay agenda.[29]

Our LGBTQ+ neighbors desire to be seen, heard, given space to breathe, and to express love in the ways that they understand that God has

---

29. Ó Tuama, *Love is the Great Endeavor*, 14.

put into their hearts. The people we heard in this chapter chronicled many concrete ways of showing love in the conversation above. They tell us that:

- Love is not the same thing as niceness. Niceness and harm can coexist in a person. Ignoring this actually makes it more likely for harm to continue to occur. We need to be more concerned about what our actions do to other people than we are about whether or not they think we are nice.

- Love is choosing to, at the very least, not be rejecting. We can choose to see the LGBTQ+ person as a gift we can learn from, an image bearer of the divine. We can accept them human to human, regardless.

- Love is trying even if we don't know how. Love is trying to use the preferred pronouns (he/him, she/her, they/them, something else). Love is trying to avoid using heterosexist language (are you dating someone rather than do you have a boyfriend). Love is recognizing and accepting when we get it wrong (without always trying to defend ourselves), learning, and trying again. Love keeps trying.

- Love is doing our own homework. We can look up terms we don't yet know. We can look up tips to work on our language. We can read books by people about their experiences as LGBTQ+. We can be open to getting to know LGBTQ+ Christians. We can make the choice to not avoid the topic due to discomfort (and real risk even to allies in some faith communities) but to explore the source of that discomfort and risk and dig into the questions or the concerns that we carry

- Love is not making this the one thing that is the deal-breaker. Love looks to one's gifts and strengths and all of the other things we know about the LGBTQ+ person. It looks to the fruits of love in a person's life. Love makes room and asks questions regarding pertinent things beyond sexual identity and orientation. Love looks to the whole person.

- Love is not putting up with hate speech or mistreatment toward anyone at any time. In any room with twenty or more people, the likelihood is that at least one identifies as LGBTQ+.[30] Love does not need to know that there is an LGBTQ+ identifying person in the room in order to call out hate speech.

30. Gushee, *Changing Our Mind*, 46.

- And perhaps the root of them all, love is not talking at, but listening. Deeply.

Ó Tuama asserts:

> The church cannot continue to speak about us AND define the parameters of acceptable response to their words. If the church wants to speak about us in this way, where questions are cast upon the morality of our love, then the church at large needs to have the courage to say: "We will have the moral courage to ask you how it feels to be spoken about in this way, and we will believe that you are telling us the truth when you give us feedback." This would be a real listening process. Currently the church at large wants to say "we are saying this about you" and "here is how you should feel about it." This is not listening at all.[31]

Real love does not talk at; it talks with. This requires having the courage to listen to what the other has to say in response. It requires being in the same room together.

To listen is to think about another's experience. It is also to consider how the questions and pressures they regularly experience would affect us if we were in their shoes. Ó Tuama offers two examples of good listening in this way. He talks about a woman he spoke with, "a moderately conservative Christian, who said 'I would hate to have my relationship with my husband questioned in the way I question your relationship with your partner.'"[32] In making this statement, she considered her thoughts and their implications if she were to ask them of herself and her own relationship. This is a step toward love.

Another example Ó Tuama offers is a man who asked, "What's it like for you when you hear me say that I am welcoming of you, but not affirming of you?"[33] Again, here is an example of owning one's own limitations and demonstrating real concern to hear how those impact another's life. This man knows that his position holds potential contradictions. He shows genuine concern for how those contradictions impact his LGBTQ+ neighbor's life. This is a component to listening. It is a step toward love. It may be uncomfortable in a world of confirmation bias where we have the option to be surrounded by opinions that are often echoing our own. But risking

31. Ó Tuama, *Welcoming the Neighbor*, 2.

32. Ó Tuama, "A Lived Theology of Listening," 16.

33. Ibid.

discomfort for the sake of love may just be the way to discovering not only real love, but also real truth in the process.

Kori writes in her bit entitled, "On where I am theologically: I'm not comfortable, but I don't miss my comfortable."[34] Stepping out behind interpretations that no longer hold us together and risking the discomfort of authentic, faithful, and responsible interpretation together may not bring a new comfort as quick as we want. But quick is not the goal. Neither is comfort. Love is.

We can do these things. We do not have to throw out the Bible in order to care for our LGBTQ+ neighbors. We may need to look to it with tools wider and deeper than what current debates suggest. Our LGBTQ+ neighbors bring and are powerful gifts to the church and to the world. When we refuse to listen to them, we miss out on these gifts. We miss out on crucial questions and stories about human experience and about the nature of God and love in the world. We miss out on questions and perspectives that may even help us to understand our own sacred realities better. For as Ó Tuama reminds us: "This is not a question of whether we keep the gospel or dilute the gospel. This is a question of whether we are more fully turned toward the gospel. To turn toward, to listen to and learn from the LGBT members of the Church . . . is an invitation to love God more, love the gospel more, and to love truth more. Let us join each other on this great endeavor."[35]

So, say it with me:

> "*Leader:* Be brave
> *All:* Because you are a child of God
> *Leader:* And be kind
> *All:* Because so is everyone else"[36]

34. DeSimone, "On Where I Am Theologically."

35. Ó Tuama, from the blog on "Love is the Great Endeavor—Audio and Text."

36. Martin, *UnClobber*, 147.

5

There's No Guarantee I'll Make it Home at Night

Short Leashes, Color-Blindness, and Being a Young Black Man in the US Today

"Wait. Mamma?" My then six-year-old son looked up, confusion and fresh alarm on his face. He had wandered in to where I was listening to the Grand Jury's verdict regarding the shooting of Michael Brown in Ferguson, Missouri.

"Yeah, bud," I said back, meeting his gaze and trying to make the concern on my own face soften.

"Did they say that a police officer shot and killed somebody? I thought police were supposed to keep us safe." His question was one of those potentially paradigm-shifting ones. My sister-in-law is a cop. She is also one of his favorite people on the planet. The statement simply did not compute with his perception of the profession through his relationship with her. I think he knew there were high stakes in asking it. I definitely knew there were high stakes in choosing how to respond.

"I know, buddy. That's what they're talking about. Something went wrong and people are trying to figure out what went wrong. It wasn't supposed to be like this."

Conversations like this happened all over the US on that evening. And I suspect that conversations in households with little boys who look a lot like Michael Brown went differently than the one with my son.

My son is white. Our family is predominantly white. The narratives and experiences in white middle-class communities about and with the police are different than those in many other communities. I have never had to have "the talk"[1] with my white son regarding his interactions with the police in the same ways that my friends and colleagues of color have. I regularly have the talk with my son about recognizing and bearing the privilege that his whiteness and maleness and US citizenship bring in the world. But that conversation does not carry the same kind of existential fear that undergirds it as a parent. Mine is a fear of him perpetuating systems of injustice that continue to communicate a hierarchy that some people belong and others do not. My fear carries a hope for a different future and a grief for the structures that continue to prefer some to others. It recognizes the lottery that my son has won, through no merit of his own, and attempts to grow responsibility within him and a thirst for justice along with it. It is not the fear of whether or not he will come home every time he leaves the house. My "talk" does not bring the same stakes with it that the parents of children of color experience.

THE FRAME

It is easy to shut down a conversation about race with white folks by talking about the history of racial injustice in our country. You may hear comments like, "but that was then and this is now." You may hear comments like, "but I am not my colonizing or slave-owning ancestors. What do you want me to do about something that happened so long ago that I didn't have anything to do with?" You may hear statements like, "but we had an African American President." Those statements might be true, in a sense. They also do not change anything. And events erupting all over the country in recent years in Ferguson, Baltimore, Dallas, Standing Rock, Charleston, New York, Charlottesville, etc. remind us that something is going on, whether people in predominantly white communities understand it or want to talk about it or not. For people holding on to a foundation of neighbor-love, we need to pay attention.

1. Hear Clint Smith's TEDTalk on "How to Raise a Black Son in America" here: *https://www.ted.com/talks/clint_smith_how_to_raise_a_black_son_in_america.*

History is not the whole of the story. But it is important. And the history of the US includes systematic discrimination against people of color, including people of African descent. This has occurred via institutionalized human enslavement, lynching, segregation, displacement, structural discrimination in employment and housing (among other things), and is now raising its head in the disproportionate realities of mass incarceration, the "school to prison pipeline," and questions around police involved violence and the just-ness of the justice system. To deny this is to deny a reality of our country. To say, "but that was then and this is now" or "but what did I do?" is to dismiss the sustained trauma experienced by human beings then and now in a country that was built on these structures and that often tries to ignore them rather than dismantle them. There are many books and films that chronicle pieces of this history.[2] If you are unfamiliar with it and/or if you are hungry or brave enough to know more, I recommend that you start there.

History is not the whole of the story. This is also a story of harmful theologies, which is all the more reason why people of faith need to take this work and these questions seriously. From using the possibility to introduce people to Christianity as a reason to justify colonization and enslavement, to identifying people of African descent as only three-fifths of a person and not fully the image of God, to categorizing races and nationalities into a "great chain of being" hierarchically placing people of European descent as highest and closest to angels and people of African descent closer to animals, to creating theologies that justified these systems by identifying darker skin as "the curse of Ham," theologies have always been a part of this story, and not innocently so.[3] There have been white allies and accomplices in many of the stages of this story. They have and continue to advocate for the recognition of the full humanity and dignity of people of color. There have also been crowds of people leaving Sunday church to participate in a public murder by lynching of one of their black neighbors. And there have been multitudes of people in the white church that have simply remained silent, either because they/we did not feel impacted enough to act and speak or because they/we simply did not know what to say or do. People of faith have always been a part of how the story takes shape. That means we are and can be part of the story of how it takes shape in our time and for the future.

One of the challenges people in the white church face is that for many of us, the gospel has been narrowed to a nearly exclusively personal one.

2. For a place to begin, see the Appendix.
3. To read more, see Trentaz, *Theology in the Age of AIDS & HIV.*

Lisa Sharon Harper in *The Very Good Gospel,* summarizes the way we sometimes hear the gospel described as: "God loves us, but we're sinful. As a result, we're separated from God. Jesus died to pay the penalty for our sins. All we have to do is believe that his death was enough and we get to go to heaven."[4] Harper comments that sure, that is good news because "who wants to languish in hell forever?" However, reflecting on an experience she had while walking through the King Center in Atlanta, seeing the abuses and trials that people of color have experienced in our country, she states, "one thought haunted me: *The good news of my gospel doesn't feel good enough.*"[5]

The gospel formula sometimes reads as: God sent Jesus to save me from my sins, so if I confess my sins and ask him into my heart, God will forgive and I will spend eternity with God. Our task between that initial prayer and the "heavenly reward" is then to try to be a good person and live a sinless life. Even sin is largely identified in personal, individual categories. In terms of the social dimension of it all, we are to give charitably to those who are "the least of these" and worship together and be in community with each other in sorting out what it all means. When you look at it closely, however, the central component is still an individualized gospel that is celebrated in community. What does this good news say in the face of human enslavement? Is this good news good enough? Is this the whole of the good news as revealed in the life and teachings of Jesus?

Harper, leaning into the question that haunted her, challenged her team members to dig into Matthew, Mark, Luke, and John for the question "What exactly *was* Jesus's 'good news'?" What they found was that the Gospel writers "all cared about an individual's reconciliation with God, self, and their communities." Check. And, "the gospel writers also focused on systemic justice, peace between people groups, and freedom for the oppressed. The good news was both about the *coming* of the Kingdom of God and the *character* of that Kingdom."[6]

This is consistent with many throughout history. As I mentioned in chapter 1, Wesleyan theologians, social gospelers, and liberation theologians of many stripes, to name a few in recent-ish history, have recognized the significant social dimensions of following Jesus that go along with the personalized dimensions. Caring for our neighbors is not simply an

4. Harper, *The Very Good Gospel,* 2.
5. Ibid.
6. Harper, *The Very Good Gospel,* 6.

outgrowth of our conversion to the ways of God. It is part and parcel of our transformation toward the kin-dom of God in the world. It is part of our becoming like Jesus. It is not optional. This is something that faith communities of color have been the leaders in for centuries, a reminder of this covenant toward shalom laced all throughout the biblical text.[7] This holds a thicker both/and gospel, Harper explains, and with it, ways to hold our pieces and our lives together.

This orientation toward the world is not exclusive to theology but is also connected to, implicated in, and indicative of different perceptions of how the world works in different arenas as well. Individualistic or personalized orientation to the world leads to what many scholars call "the bootstraps model." This model is based on a belief that anyone can achieve the American Dream with enough elbow grease, hard work, determination, and, therefore, "pulling yourselves up by your own bootstraps."[8] That model of seeing the world leads to the perspective that if some people are having a harder time or if there are inequities in the social order, it is because some people are simply not working hard enough. It does not see or account for the structural dynamics of access or denied access often informed by race, class, gender, etc. It does not account for the ways biases impact policies or the ways that family access into a field increases the chances that someone else in the next generation might also follow in those footsteps (see the example of applying for college in chapter 2). When individualism becomes the litmus test or lens for our experiences, we develop an inability to see the ways that systems and structures affect opportunity in people's lives. Given the history of race in our country, it can blind us to the ways that racist structures and policies continue to have impact.

One currently hot example is illustrated by womanist biblical scholar Mitzi J. Smith in her exploration of 2 Kings 2:23–25 through the lens of police brutality. She states, "The majority of white Americans perceive that instances of police brutality can be attributed to a few rotten apples in the barrel (it is an individual problem), while others, primarily people of color, argue that the barrel is rotten (it is an institutional or systemic problem)."[9] This marked difference in viewing the world represents a marked difference in experiencing it. Communities of color have experienced disproportionate

7. See Brueggemann, *Peace.*

8. For a very succinct definition of the bootstraps model and its implications in people's experience, see Matsushima, "The Struggles of Discussing Race."

9. Smith, M., *Womanist Sass and Talk Back,* 95.

officer involved violence, with Native Americans and African Americans topping the statistics.[10] When your experiences are different, your questions and perspectives on what is going on will be, too. This difference in perspective on individual vs. structural dynamics may begin to explain the conflict between experiencing people as "nice" or "good" people while still seeing racist, sexist, and/or homophobic behaviors from them. It also begins to explain the absence of many white communities from challenging and dismantling structures and policies that favor certain communities. This is not only a difference with political implications. It has theological implications as well.

This raises some significant questions for those of us in the "white church." What is it that has kept our ancestors silent for centuries in the face of injustices? What is it that keeps us silent now? Do we still hold ideologies that say that people of color are not as human as we are, not as much in the image of God? Where do those ideas come from? Where have they been a part of the messages we absorb in our families, our communities, our churches? To whom do we tend to give the benefit of the doubt? To whom do we not offer that same benefit? What are the thoughts or emotions that raise up when we are with or see our neighbors of color and, in our time, young African American men in particular? Where do those come from?

These questions are not questions for a quick "checking off" and moving to the next. They are questions that need asked to bring what is sometimes unconscious into our consciousness. It does not make us "bad people" to begin to realize that we hold biased perspectives. It may make us "bad people" to ignore them and continue to behave out of our own ignorance. And it certainly creeps on "bad" if we are more concerned about our "goodness or badness" than we are about how our neighbors of color are treated in the world.

It is important to recognize that these ideas have not simply always been there as a part of the "divine truth" of how the world works, but, particularly in the US, were a part of creating and maintaining the economic fabric of this country, beginning with the systemically unjust treatment of people indigenous to the Americas and widening to include other people of color.[11] They get passed down in policies and structures so that many of us in white communities simply do not have to question our root beliefs

10. Hanson, "The Forgotten Minority."

11. For more on these dynamics, see Wytsma, *The Myth of Equality* or Wallis, *America's Original Sin.*

and inherent biases around race nor challenge the systems that feed and sustain them (and keep them invisible to us). That is not the case for our friends and neighbors of color. Their experiences have given them eyes to see dimensions of the world to which we can be blind. This is not easy work. Yet, our "not knowing" is neither a reason to be frozen with guilt, nor is it reason to remain in our not knowing. We need to give up some of our definitions of "goodness." We need to be more concerned with the wellbeing of those who are being harmed than with our own reputations in certain spaces. Shiny, clean, doing everything right according to what I have been told may not be an option. That is also not the model I see in Jesus's life and ministry.

I have spent years trying to recognize the privilege I have and to see the ways that I act that play into a racist system and reveal my own short-comings. I still mess up. And I do not expect easy grace or forgiveness when I do. For the difficulty of my journey is only a fraction of the burden carried by my colleagues of color.[12] This is not a pity party for any of us. For falling into feelings of guilt or shame or pity are counterproductive in that they often allow us to stay in that space, or seek a quick way out, rather than the long-term work of seeking justice and life in the world for us all. Guilt is not our goal; love is. Our work is toward shalom, the kin-dom of God, life abundant for ourselves and our neighbors, not soothed consciences or intact egos.

This is hard work. It is deep work. As Leroy Barber reminds us, "God can handle the struggle of the deep; our shallowness is what's really killing us."[13] The thin-ness of our gospel and of our perceptions of the world is killing us. It does not have to be like this.

This work has not begun, nor will it end with us. This has already been cross-generational work. That does not mean that we give in to the cries of "slow down, not that way, be reasonable and patient" that white allies inside and outside of the church have far too often uttered.[14] And we cannot settle for abstract love from a distance. Rather, engaging race in our country right now requires a love that risks, a love that does what it takes to show the beloved that they are loved.

But we are getting ahead of ourselves. So how do you love across these kinds of divisions with centuries of history and theological momentum?

12. See Brown, *I'm Still Here.*

13. Barber, *Embrace,* 26.

14. See King, "Letter from Birmingham Jail," for one poignant example.

THE CONVERSATIONS

All people of color experience pressures in our country. However, the messages about young African American men have played a particular role in our current national psyche. So, I spent some time listening to a group of young men of color, all in their 20s, primarily African American and bi-racial (but I will also highlight some voices of Latinx and Indigenous men as their experiences confirm many similar dynamics), about the complexities of racial dynamics in the US right now through the lens of their experiences and what feels like love to them.

We started the conversation simply talking about what it is like to be a young black man in the US right now, what pressures they face, and what messages about themselves they absorb. The first thing they commented on was uncertainty and fear.

Hakeem Bradley (a youth worker and pastor who takes every opportunity to walk with and inspire young people and who carries a unique and needed combination of being able to speak straight to the core of an issue and do so with power and a joy that lights up a room) starts off by saying, "life is scary because I'm a young black male who is married. And there is no guarantee I'll make it home to Jazmon at night. No guarantee. I might make a wrong turn or I might just be 'black driving'[15] and get pulled over and any wrong movement could cause me my life. That's scary. I drive every day. I'm scared that my life isn't valuable. I just don't feel like my life matters in the general public's eye." [See more about Hakeem at www.loveinatimeoffear.com and click on the video of Hakeem.]

Head nods and affirmations abound around the room. This uncertainty was shared by the other men of color as well, uncertainty about each day as well as a pervasive feeling of not belonging, of always having to watch their backs. And with the feeling of not belonging comes a sense of having a "wall" they constantly have to push or climb or a "leash" that pulls them back.

Montel Shirley (a recent college grad with a pride in his community and passion to help via a career in juvenile corrections, whose own story fuels him, and whose whole demeanor communicates quiet strength and discipline along with a rascally shy smile) jumps in, "personally, being African American, I don't think I'm presented the same opportunities as other

---

15. "Black driving" or "driving while black" refers to the perceptions and experiences of African American drivers of being pulled over more often than their white counter parts.

people. I think people of color can be just as qualified as other people and still not get the same opportunities as others get."

Da'Lorian Sampson (a goal-oriented, family-oriented college student, driven, deep thinker and question-asker) chimes in with affirmations, "I just feel like, as African Americans, we have a hold to what we can do. There's a limit that we can't surpass. I feel like it's been like that for years. And we're still trying to figure out a way to get over that hump."

Their experiences are in direct opposition to the bootstraps model.

Montel gives an example from his own life, "I know I wasn't supposed to be one of the guys that necessarily graduated from college and received a bachelor's degree. I feel like our leash is a little bit shorter, you know? I feel like I have no room for error." He comments on the fact that the label is that young African American men are "always getting into trouble," so, in carrying this, Montel continues, "wherever I go I have someone watching."

Da'Lorian finishes his thought, "I feel like white Americans get more opportunities and multiple but I feel like for us, we have to be ready for our opportunity and if it passes us, it just goes on to the next person. We always have to be ready." These guys have not always experienced second chances. They know they are not guaranteed.

Victor Gallardo-Molina (who we met in chapter 2), confirms that these feelings are consistent with many Latinx men as well. "I think the hardships that I've been through have given me a mindset where I know I've got to work double, triple as hard as other people. I know I have to put in double and triple the time to get to the same place as other people. I know I have to prepare myself more than the average person has to for anything. I think, at the end of the day, the value you learn is work harder. Work harder than most people just to achieve maybe possibly the same success, which is totally fine, because at the end of the day, the feeling is a lot more rewarding when you achieve something knowing how hard you worked your butt off for it."

These brilliant and courageous young men talk about how that has helped them in many cases. They have worked hard to be disciplined, to practice their skills, to be excellent in what they do. They have lots of practice in showing up and being cool and ready for whatever the opportunity is. As Victor states, "You grow up kind of used to it."

However, they also talk about the toll it takes on a person to always be in that hyper-vigilant state, something that is reinforced by trauma and resiliency studies. These men share about how exhausting it can be to constantly need to prove you are as good as others, that you belong here, that you are gifted in all the right ways and to do it without a touch of arrogance or intensity that could be taken as aggression. This carries into so many arenas of life so that even in a space that is not majority white, they talked about still feeling minoritized and "leashed" as young African American men in particular.

Josh Thomas (a recent college grad who embodies a story of overcoming expectations and circumstances along with his remarkable wife, Amari, a genuine, loving, and leads-with-the-heart kind of guy who Hakeem described by saying, "even the way that dude blinks is cool") talks about it this way, "you have to present yourself a certain way. I feel like sometimes with a group of whites or going for a certain job, we have to talk a certain way; if we get upset about something we have to hold it in and don't get to express how we feel."

There are at least two dynamics here in the need to code-switch—to change how one talks, walks, presents oneself depending on the company you are in—in order to be "respectable" or recognized as professional, well-behaved, intelligent, or "worthy." Often these models are patterned after white cultural ways of being and, therefore, serve to reinforce a sense of not belonging or feeling "othered" or "less than" for these men. My friend, JR Lilly, speaking from his experiences of navigating these realities as a Navajo man, refers to it as "another form of imperialism." And many of these men have also become masterful at it.

Hakeem adds to this, speaking of the "expectation to conform to the dominant culture" in most of his work environments, all of which have been "majority white," and discussing some of the implications of this beyond respectability but also extending to love. In his experience, the feeling is, "when I conform to your culture, then I'm included into this love circle that's going on . . . and if I do anything that's contrary to this culture, then I'm non-deserving of being loved." These implications are part of why Hakeem refuses to play the code-switching game. Being authentic is important to him. "The only time I do flip the switch is when I have to turn off certain things that I just know universally won't be understood."

Others don't always feel that luxury. Ryan Jackson (a college student and natural networker who embodies a combination of energetic and laid back, bubbly on the surface, but who has learned to guard some of the deeper pieces of himself) talks about the ways his bi-racial identity shapes him as a "mix of everything" and also forces him to feel like he straddles two different worlds. "For me, it's interesting because, being mixed, I have kind of both sides. It almost feels really weird just being in the middle of two sides that are clashing right now. Being halfway in a privileged white space, I had a good school. I had most of the same opportunities. When I am hanging out with my black friends, I act a certain way and we get looks from people just because we're loud and rambunctious and just who we are. There are certain times when I can act that way and certain times when I have to change how I act. I had to learn how to switch between almost two alter egos and so it kind of makes you feel like you're not either one of them. You kind of feel like out of place." His biracial identity, in some ways, helps him to see even more clearly the racial dynamics at play in shaping our experiences.[16]

Ryan continues telling about how he learned the need to switch from watching his dad's business interactions, especially when dealing with white clients. He remembers his dad telling him, "this is something you've got to do because you can't be 'all black because that will scare them off.'" But Ryan says that for him, as bi-racial, the switching is not only for business or professional settings, but he feels the pressure to switch while with different friend groups as well. When he is with his white friends, he continues, "I have to act a little blacker than them; and when I'm with my black friends, I definitely have to be black. I feel like there's almost more pressure to be black for me, especially because black is trendy and black is cool. If I was more stereotypical black I would probably get less weird looks. As soon as your skin is a color people expect you to act that color."

Implied in Ryan's last comment is that even when playing "by the rules," one's appearance carries certain narratives with it in the wider culture. Switching cannot completely erase those. Josh affirms this in reflecting on the pressure to hold in his feelings whereas for others there is a sense like, "well, they're upset so that's why they acted the way they did and it's understandable." However, for young African American men, Josh continues, "It's like we're out of control or feared most of the time. I think fear would be the biggest issue. Cops pull their guns first on African Americans because they feel we're dangerous."

The conversation turned to the recent gunman in a school shooting in Florida, a young white man who was taken into custody by the police

---

16. This reminds me of the TEDx talk by Paula Stone Williams, a trans-woman, who talks about her experiences living both as a man in the US and now as a woman and how formerly invisible realities of sexism have become very clear to her: *https://www.youtube. com/watch?v=lrYx7HaUlMY.*

alive. "That would never happen," Josh continues, "we get shot down for juice and candy."

Fear is present in the lives of these young men. Fear makes people dangerous as it makes us more likely to act with impulse rather than careful deliberation. The dominant messages being absorbed by others to fear African American men have, therefore, created a life where they themselves have to constantly live with fear, regardless of how diligent and disciplined and thoughtful they are.

Da'Lorian tells a story of mistaken identity from his own experience. "[The police] stopped us because they got a call that two African American males were walking the same way we were walking and the call was that they had guns on them. So they stopped us, searched us, frisked us. They just assumed that it was us and at that time I felt anger because that could happen to anyone and the situation could have been worse for us if we didn't want to cooperate or if we had something else to say to them. It could've escalated to something else."

This knowing of what "could've been" is ever-present for these young men. And for their parents.

So is their pride in their racial-ethnic heritage and the African American community.

Hakeem keys in on this as, after talking about his fears, he adds, "on the flip side of that, my life is also dope being black. I wouldn't want to be any other ethnicity because we set the trend on what's cool musically, athletically, style-wise."

"Then it gets taken from us," Josh interjects.

"And then we come up with something new," Hakeem offers with his signature laugh. "I come from a very innovative people. We create and innovate and influence." He continues, "I think dominant culture loves black culture but wouldn't want the experience of being black."

That statement and the mention of athletics spurs another round of reflection as this is a group of college athletes. The labels that athletes sometimes carry in our society have complicated their experiences in additional ways.

Montel reflects that, "with sports in general, I have no room for any bad sportsmanship. The label on us is we tend to be a little more aggressive than others." Those labels follow them on the streets, in the classroom, and on the court.

Ryan adds, "Sometimes people think you're getting special treatment. Especially since we play sports that are identified with our culture, that even brings into more stereotypes of who we are in the classroom and who we are in general. I'm studying psychology so I've been thinking a lot about this, but there's a way that when people put an identity on you and you're receiving it from a lot of people, it becomes you. Just because I'm a basketball player, and maybe because I'm black, I don't know, they expect me to be lazy or to not show up."

School has been a place where a lot of the pressures and stereotypes have shown up for this group of men. It has also been a place where they have experienced both examples of love that felt like love to them and examples of good intentions that missed and even caused harm. They talk about three major categories in particular of efforts that missed: over-helping (helping when help was not needed), forced transactional relationships (relationships that seemed to have an agenda other than getting to know them), and "color-blindness" on matters of race.

Several of the men express how excited they usually are to enter into educational spaces for the first time and how that excitement deflates when they discover early that stereotypes have preceded them and their teachers or administration have already decided how well they will do and/or who they are or aren't. Regardless of whether or not teachers or administrators intentionally build spaces that communicate those things, that is the perception and message that these men express regularly experiencing. In their stories, that has not always meant that people have given up on them as fill in the blank with all the stereotypes and labels we hear about young men of color. It also shows up from people who think they are actively fighting against systems of injustice to care for them.

Ryan tells his story this way. "I haven't had the best school record ever but I'm not dumb." He pauses and laughs at his next response with honesty, saying, "I'm just lazy." He continues, "so people would talk to me and it would look like they were trying to help me but it made me feel like they were looking at me as the outcast. I was a black kid, a mixed kid, in a predominantly white school. They would ask me, 'do you have dyslexia? Do you have a learning disability?' And I know they were probably trying to help but it wasn't received that way."

This was consistent with the Latinx men I spoke with as well. Fernando Ibanez (a quiet observant, deep thinking soccer player who always has something important to contribute but who doesn't always have the invitation to share it) adds, "I remember growing up when they put you in special reading programs or writing programs. I feel like at times I could read or write better than some of the kids that were born here. I remember I didn't need ESL anymore past third or fourth grade but in middle school they were still trying to have me go into it."

Fernando gives another example, "In high school there was a drug free program and I remember I was always invited to those. I don't have any stories to share about drugs. I had no reason to go in, but by asking us to go in it was like saying, 'you guys need this.'" They invited mostly young men of color, Fernando adds.

He was quick to point out that these dynamics are not just in their lives, but have been consistent in his parents' experience as well. "I know that for my mom," Fernando begins, "once we got here, we didn't have a lot of money to support ourselves so she used assistance from different programs. She was really thankful for that. But even now she still gets asked, 'hey, if you need help on rent or whatever.' When that happens, my mom feels like she is still in that cycle where every person of color can't progress." Assumptions can cause harm. Even those with good intentions.

Montel and Da'Lorian have similar yet slightly different takes on the subject. They talk about coming up against some obstacles in their educational journeys and having advisors or teachers come alongside and immediately try to help them brainstorm other options. That might sound like someone showing love and care, but to Montel and Da'Lorian, it feels more like pity.

Montel explains it this way, "those who are coming up to me out of pity try to give alternative options. Those who know me would be sincere, would try to support me and tell me 'that's something you would be great at,'" referring to his dreams and paths he wants to pursue. He adds, "if you give someone an alternative option it sounds like not listening to my dream."

Da'Lorian finishes the thought, "it sounds like they want you to find the easy way out instead of, you know, going through the trials and tribulations of going through the path that you want. That's not fair to us because everybody [at home] is telling us to go make our dream a reality but you're telling us to take the easy way out. How are we supposed to go for what we want if we're always told to take the easy way out?"

The way to avoid that, these men agree, is to get to know them. Ask questions. Find out what their dreams are, what the exact obstacle is, and help them to figure out strategies to work through it rather than go around it. Do not assume that you know what the problem is, but ask questions to really listen to how they see it so that you can also really listen to what might be helpful next steps. These men are models of strength and determination and creative problem solving. They have had to be rock stars at it their entire lives. In essence, their word to us is, do not fall prey to the "white savior" complex. These men have what they need within them. They do not need people to swoop in and make it all better. Sometimes they simply need a partner who has been familiar with "the system" to come alongside, and to genuinely come alongside them, not our imagined picture of who they are and what they need. They want us to do so out of care for them, not in order to make them a piece in our bigger strategy of overturning systems or soothing our guilty consciences. This leads into another area where well-intentioned people have "missed it" with these men—forced transactional relationships.

Montel tells stories of people coming up to him at college in a way that felt forced, like people were trying to get to know him, but for something. He talks about people who seemed to try to engage him because he is quieter in class. Often, he says that started to look like "support out of pity," either because of assumptions about what he did or did not understand in class (reinforcing some of the stereotypes listed above) or because people assumed certain things about his background. He also shares stories about people approaching him because he is "a minority," but does not come across as aggressive, therefore circling back to labels discussed earlier. "That hurts me," Montel states matter of factly.

Not talking in class does not have to mean that people do not understand. It does not have to mean that people are not interested. It also does not have to be an invitation for further relationship. It could mean that someone is an introvert, an internal processer, or not feeling willing to share their thoughts out loud with the class for a number of different reasons. That is as true about black men as about other people. But these particular men feel that they have not always gotten that benefit of the doubt.

Another element of the transactional relationships is when, as Josh put it, people "feel like they have to sugar-coat things with the intention that you won't get so angry." Sugar-coating brings a feeling of patronizing or paternalism. It feels like talking down. It also serves as a reminder that you are afraid of them getting angry. That means that you might be afraid of them, period. Then you are back at the stereotypes again.

As Da'Lorian put it, "if you keep it honest, sincere, and straight with people, it'll go a lot further than sugar-coating and having fear. If you keep it honest, we have no other way to take it but to respect that. To sugar-coat it only makes it worse. That's where the anger comes out."

We get into a little conversation about "white fragility."[17] These men are so used to being blamed for escalation and, therefore, shouldering the responsibility for others staying calm because they have so often been faced with systems that assume they are the aggressor. That should not be on them. What I heard in these conversations, although they said it gently, was the desire to be free to be human, to be able to express what they feel and think, and have that received as legitimate. Then, when there are questions or "push back" about what they feel and think, to do so honestly and thoughtfully and not with fear that they will "lose control."

What they are mostly asking is for people to want to be in a relationship with them because they are amazing human beings not because someone wants help to become less racist or to help change the world (although both may happen in the context of a real relationship). In other words, make the relationship a relationship, not a transaction. That might mean that we have to hear hard things about ourselves, the world, and our place in it. Given this, it would benefit us all to do our own work, especially if our social worlds have not been very racially diverse up to this point. Things to help us do that work are readily accessible.

Austin Channing Brown, in an interview regarding her recent book, *I'm Still Here,* affirms this by saying:

> White folks need to take a step back instead of seeking out that friend, that person who's going to teach them. They should seek out education, seek out books, seek out spaces where people of color are willing to talk, seek out the lecture, seek out the class, seek out the book studies. Seek out the spaces where people of color have already agreed to share their stories with you. That way when you come into proximity with people of color, you will have a larger foundation to build a relationship as opposed to using me

17. At its basics, Robin DiAngelo, the white professor who established the term, defined it as, "a state in which even a minimum amount of racial stress becomes intolerable, triggering a range of defensive moves. These moves include the outward display of emotions such as anger, fear, and guilt, and behaviors such as argumentation, silence, and leaving the stress-inducing situation." You can read more at the Oxford Dictionaries blog post discussing this term as well as find a link to that original article: *https://blog.oxforddictionaries.com/2017/12/15/white-fragility-word-of-the-year-2017-shortlist/.*

as your teacher. The goal of our friendship shouldn't be for me to
be your teacher. It should be me as your friend.[18]

Doing this homework will also help to avoid the third major category
of missing it—claiming to be color-blind. As Hakeem said, "being color-
blind is not a thing. Yeah, there's an aspect about not letting someone's skin
tone make your decisions, but to say you're color-blind is to negate somebody's experience, to negate their culture, to negate part of them. You know
what I mean? To negate my blackness? What do you mean? It's my struggle.
It's my life. So to deny my blackness is to deny me. I just think it's stupid and
it perpetuates the system. It doesn't negate racism, it enables it."

So, what are examples of getting it right? How have people shown love
in ways that connected as love? What looks, sounds, and/or feels like love
to these men?

All of them had examples of people who took the time to really get to
know them. Ryan talks about moments when teachers saw him for who he
is and what he could be. "They just didn't give up on me. They had a meeting with me and told me, 'you're smarter than this. I know you can be doing
better, I'm going to give you another chance.' I remember in that class, I had
an F at midterm and ended with a B. I was able to pass the class and also
learned a lot. Just don't give up on them and you've got to really reach out
and stop the kid after class because, when you're in a system like we are,
even if you're reaching out through email, it's not personal and we kind of
read it and are like, 'whatever,' but the more personal it is, you can feel the
care and it's time to put some work in." The more direct and personal the
contact, although without pushing, the more like love it feels.

Fernando echoes this as well, talking about a teacher who helped him
figure out how to navigate thinking about and applying for college, even
paying for summer school when Fernando had a difficult year after a good
friend died. She contacted him all summer. She checked in on him. She
made sure he was eating while his parents had to work long hours. She
would call to make sure he got home. That consistency and the refusal to
give up on him meant a ton to Fernando. "And I passed and was even able
to play soccer my senior year and it was a time when I was unsure what I
wanted to do and I did have that temptation to try things, but she would
say, 'I know what you're capable of.' She believed in me." And she showed it.

Many of the men talk about people who continually proved that they
cared about them. They are tired of people who claim care but then make

18. Austin Channing Brown qtd. in Miller, "Austin Channing Brown."

them reach out to get it. They are too smart for that. They have seen too much for that. If we want to show them that we mean it, then we will keep showing up. It might take a while, but they will notice that showing up.

Another way of demonstrating love has been the willingness to ask questions. Da'Lorian says it this way, "it's really about having your own experience. If you want to know about someone's race, ask questions. It's about how you have the conversation. If someone wants to know about me and my background, I would rather you have a sit down and just ask me questions. I know you may not understand or know how to ask but at least you're trying and you want to know yourself rather than judging."

Ryan affirms this as well saying, "One thing I wish my grandparents would do is ask 'what is it like for you?' instead of taking it all from Fox news. Sometimes they make remarks that they don't fully understand. If you're going to have some kind of relationship, get where you're coming from and try to understand that there's a different sort of background and I'm not what all my labels say I am. I'm much deeper than that."

Hakeem also affirms this, "The best interaction is when somebody asks questions, like what you're doing right now. That feels like love because when people genuinely ask questions who are of dominant culture about who I am, my experiences, what I think, and how all of that has shaped who I am, I go, bro, okay, this is what it looks like to build relationships. You ask these questions and you get to know each other. When they do that to me, I just go, wow, there are people who genuinely care and want to learn. And that is love." He continues, commenting on moments when he has talked with people who disagree with him on various issues or on his perspective of the world. Rather than simply telling someone they're wrong, Hakeem suggests, say, "tell me more. Why do you feel like that? Being understood is how I feel loved."

Not everyone is willing to be our teacher. That is simply not their job. However, many of these men welcome legitimate interest and care. Something many of these men shared was the need to be curious and to look deeper. Montel adds, "be mindful and not easily influenced by other people. Be vulnerable in a way to hearing and listening without easily judging. Experience it first. Try to understand. Just look at it, just for a little bit, from their shoes."

Da'Lorian adds, "don't take things to heart. Don't feel like I'm sitting there talking to you as if you're the problem or the one who did it but be open-minded." We may think "it wasn't me" or "it's not my problem," out of feeling defensive, but it is also very clearly not their problem to calm our feelings of guilt. Rather, these men suggest we listen to what is going on within us. Pay attention to our discomfort and try to figure out where that is coming from and how to work through it by hearing the experience of another person. This is a theme running throughout all of these chapters.

Love, for Josh, involves sacrifice and "emotional investment." It also might include things such as time and money and other resources to show concrete support. As Da'Lorian says, "people that show love will sacrifice for you. It's not always about money but if you can sacrifice your time and effort for somebody, that's love."

Josh gives an example of a moment of concrete sacrificial love in his own life in recent years. When he and Amari moved to the city where they now live they moved in with a friend who "up and left" leaving them homeless. "I came home and couldn't get into the house. The Landlord had changed the locks and all of our stuff was inside. It was 2:00AM and Amari called Matt [her basketball coach, a white man] and he said, 'all right, come to our house.' He gave us the address. We got there and they had a bed set up for us. Our thought was, 'all right, we'll stay here until we find somewhere else to live.' We ended up staying for two years. They cleaned out the basement and turned it into a little studio for us, didn't charge us rent, and ever since then they've become family to us." That experience had benefits beyond just for Amari's and Josh's housing needs. Josh continued, "it also opened our eyes to people outside of our race. They made us feel that not all white people are against us and that's when we started opening up to the community and that helped us big time because we could've ended up back home with the same people that I was trying to get away from and not finished school. But they helped us. And now we're making honest people of ourselves." The last comment, tongue in cheek, poking at the messages they often hear about themselves, causes the rest of the group to erupt in laughter.

Listen. Ask questions. Be willing to change. Be willing to show up in surprising and sometimes sacrificial ways. And, adds Hakeem, "be consistent." He refers to a moment where the men's basketball team engaged in conversations about whether or not and in what ways they would participate in the national anthem protests that occurred with athletes all over the country. "We had a long conversation going through all the pros and cons before the anthem protest, but what upset me was an understanding of 'I'm for what you're doing'" at first, but then "it felt like, but when it gets scary, we're not going to do this." He talks about which places they were allowed to do it and which places the coaches or administration had decided it would not be wise to do it. Hakeem continues, "I get there's potential danger, but when has there not been? When does it become okay to pull away from stuff? I see the good heart of not wanting us to be hurt, but I'm hurt by you not letting us do this."

Josh finishes his thought, in moments like those, it comes across "as not fear for us, but fear for them." Love, they are saying, feels like showing up in support even in moments that are scary and taking our cues from them on whether or not they want protected or accompanied.

Lastly, Ryan offers, do not put extra stuff on people that they don't need. He tells a story of going to a small school where his teachers knew a lot about his family dynamics, including his father's abuse. "I remember one time, I don't remember exactly what happened, something somewhat aggressive happened and my teacher pulled me to the side and said, 'you have to watch out because you're coming from a place of abuse and you're likely to fall back into that system.' I understand what she was saying, but as a twelve year old, that made me feel terrible. It made me feel like people were seeing me 'that way' and they didn't see me as just a kid who got mad. But because of my past, and not even my past but my father's past, they saw me as someone who was more likely to be a repeat offender."

He laments that he did not have the luxury of being received as a kid who lost his temper, but had all of the other narratives placed on top of him in interpreting that instance. He continues, "And I've never even punched somebody. I've stayed away from fights and that may be because of my past. Because when you come from a place like that, usually your one goal is to not be that." In retrospect, he describes that experience as "crushing, almost."

To close our conversation, I ask this group what final tips or piece of advice they would want to pass on and what they would want people to know about them.

Ryan offers, "We don't understand what it's like to be privileged. We don't understand what it's like to have something and then feel like it's threatened." He asked that we consider the limitations to what we know. He continues, some of us "don't understand what it's like to be in this country and then be faced with the possibility that we might have to leave. Just like we don't understand what it's like to have a father that already works at Nike so that, even if we didn't have the best schooling, boom, we still got a job at Nike paying $25/hour just because of family. I'm not condemning those families because someone, even if way back, worked for it and of course I'd love to set my kids up like that. They're trying to keep that for their family and we're not trying to take it. We're just trying to even the playing field. We're all trying to get to the place where we're financially comfortable and our families can thrive and be able to feel like we're here equally and that we all have the same sort of chance. That's what we're striving for."

Fernando adds, "It's just about family. I'm not trying to take over anything, I'm trying to share it with them."

Ryan continues, "there's a complete system of oppression and the sad part about it is that we've allowed ourselves to be oppressed because part of oppression is a mindset, but it's a lot harder and you have to do more work. For example, NBA players that came out of Compton had to say 'no' to joining a gang or say 'no' to certain things that other people said 'yes' to. The problem is that the system says, 'if you are here, this is what you do.' And if you're growing up in certain areas, you join a gang. That's what you do. If you're growing up in white suburbia, you join your father's company. That's what you do. So when that mindset gets instilled and that's what you're seeing, you get to a point where you give up hope and then are like, 'okay.' There are so many ways to get to where you want, but it's very hard work because white people are starting here," he puts his hand up at a level above his head. "And you're starting here," he continues, moving his hand to chest-level, "and you have to work like hell to get where you want. But it's a possibility."

So how do they want us to know them?

Montel states, "I'm family and goal oriented. I definitely think I'm ambitious, despite what other people say. I'm more than capable of doing what anyone else is doing. I don't need any extra help unless I personally say so. Given my background and where I'm from, that shouldn't define me. I'm proud of where I come from."

Da'Lorian offers, "I'm goal oriented, family oriented. I'm driven. I want people to know I'm responsible and, like you said, I'm capable. For me, even if I don't know something, I'm going to figure it out and I'm going to try to figure it out and if I can't, I'm going to ask for help. But I want people to know that I'm responsible and driven."

Ryan chimes in, "I would describe myself as a mix of everything. I have a side where I like to do white culture stuff like bowling or golfing, stuff like that and play video games. I have friends that are completely from white families and friends on the other side. I really feel like I'm a mixture of both of these cultures put into one."

Josh offers, "I'm a genuinely loving, quiet, but goofy guy. I care for everybody. If I meet you once and you need something, 95 percent of the time, I'm going to do what I can to help and that goes with my wife as well. Most of the time I'm quiet because I'm surveying what's around me but when I open up, I just want to make people laugh. But most of the time I don't get to share that because you have to portray yourself in certain ways in certain situations. I've been here three years but you only got to see the real me for a year and a half because I didn't feel comfortable or I didn't want to be judged. We're not dangerous. We love people. You don't have to talk to us a certain way to try to fit in. We're not going to try to rob you walking by."

Hakeem follows up with, "I'm not a threatening dude. I am not a threatening man. I want people to know that Hakeem is just a young dude who loves his wife and tries to be like Jesus. Loves Jesus, loves his wife. That's simple. That's all. We do care about our families. We have a culture that projects that black men don't care about our families. But we do."

"We love our families so much," Josh adds, "and we would do anything for our families. And if you're not blood and you become family, we'd do anything for you, too."

"We're giving people," says Da'Lorian, "even if you're not family but become family, we'll give you anything."

Hakeem takes the last word, "I am accepted by the God of this universe. That gives me peace in the midst of all the conflictions that come against me. I pray that my community can come to that understanding."

A WAY FORWARD

James Baldwin reminds us that, "American history is longer, larger, more various, more beautiful, and more terrible than anything anyone has ever said about it."[19] The experience of African Americans testifies to this. And they are not alone. Recognizing this history does not make it all of a sudden more real than it is. Rather, recognizing this history makes us more likely

---

19. Baldwin, "A Talk to Teachers." You can find the entire text at *http://richgibson .com/talktoteachers.htm* and a recent reflection on it by Clint Smith in the New Yorker at *https://www.newyorker.com/books/page-turner/james-baldwins-lesson-for-teachers-in-a -time-of-turmoil.*

to see the world as it is for many, the places of pressure as they are, and to have a fighting chance at dismantling what was built to favor some at the expense of and out of the labor of others. It does not show love to discount any portion of the terrible parts of our history or to somehow try to explain them away.

From this group of amazing, brilliant, and strong young men that I talked to, I heard that in order to show love that is received as love:

- At the very basics, we can resist the stereotypes we see and hear and get interested in them and in their lives. We can get curious about what life is like for them right now. We can get curious about what they dream about and what they are passionate about and what they are afraid of and really strive to listen and learn.

- We can do our own work. There it is again. In order to show love that is received as love, we need to honestly explore our own biases, both explicit and implicit.[20] We need to explore whether or not we are more concerned about being called racist than the implications of our behaviors for people of color. What do our actions show us? We can learn from sources and environments that are written and created to help people who are at different stages of this journey. We need to not put all of that weight of our learning or responsibility (and the potentially insensitive questions or feelings of guilt and shame along the way) on our friends or neighbors. We need to do our own work with the help of others. I will say more about this and a process we can follow in chapter 6.

- We should expect discomfort and deal with it. We need to realize that often times, it is just plain not about us. We may experience ourselves as nice or good people and still participate in systems and actions that legitimately hurt people. Learning this does not make things worse. It creates an opportunity to do and be better. Then we need to work to do and be better.

- In order to show love that feels like love, we need to fight against our "white savior complex." We are not in this relationship to save anyone from anything (other than perhaps ourselves from racist tendencies). When people of color take the risk to be in relationship with us, it is a

20. You can explore your implicit biases and associations by following the link included in the Appendix.

gift. Our job is to practice humility, gratitude, and mutuality. We have much to learn.

- Part of that means, we need to learn what it looks like to come alongside and support someone through real struggles and toward their own dreams. These may be different from our dreams for them. They may also be different than our perceptions of what is possible and what is not. Offering love means we don't look for "exit ramps" or easy solutions (for us or for them). Rather, we listen deeply to their own dreams and help them work toward them. We need to be mindful of tricky ways that racist thinking sneaks into our well-intentioned practices of trying to help. Offering easy alternatives has been one of those areas in the experiences of these young men.

- We also need to resist thinking we are farther along than we really are.

Austin Channing Brown addresses this in *I'm Still Here: Black Dignity in a World Made for Whiteness* when she says, "I am not impressed that slavery was abolished or that Jim Crow ended. I feel no need to pat America on its back for these 'achievements.' This is how it always should have been. Many call it progress, but I do not consider it praiseworthy that only within the last generation did America reach the baseline for human decency."[21]

It is not sufficient for people of faith to point to these points of "progress" in celebration and be done with it. That these "achievements" are fairly recent is a point of grief and lament and fuel for continued work toward justice and wellness and full human-ness for all people. It is not enough to take our time until the next steps pass. Young people of color in our country, our neighborhoods, homes, churches, and schools need to know that we care about them now. They need to see it with our bodies even more than they need to hear it with our mouths.

Ta-Nehisi Coates, in *Between the World and Me*, recalls a moment when he took his then thirteen-year-old son with him to work. They went to listen to a mother whose own son had recently been shot and killed. Coates recounts that he told the mother of his bafflement and anger at the verdict. He continues, "She said that she was baffled too, and that I should not mistake her calm probing for the absence of anger. But God had focused her anger away from revenge and toward redemption, she said. God had spoken to her and committed her to a new activism." Then, Coates recounts, this grieving mother turned to his own son. He states:

21. Brown, *I'm Still Here*, 151.

Then the mother of the murdered boy rose, turned to you, and said, "You exist. You matter. You have value. You have every right to wear your hoodie, to play your music as loud as you want. You have every right to be you. And no one should deter you from being you. You have to be you. And you can never be afraid to be you."[22]

This should be the message of faith communities to young people of color in our communities. How dare us ask first: What were you wearing? What did you say? How did you respond? For some of us these questions would likely be irrelevant. It is unacceptable for that to not be the case for us all. We are not all treated the same. We don't treat everyone the same. It doesn't have to be like this.

22. Coates, *Between the World and Me*, 113.

PART III

What Now?

BIT: How do we each name something we're all experiencing?

> Truth is exactly
> how you learn It,
> and still,
> likely not completely whole
>   love and no B.S.
>   K.D.[1]

"And this is my prayer, that your love may overflow more and more with knowledge and full insight," (1 Phil 1:9).

---

1. DeSimone, "How Do We Each Name Something."

6

What Now?

A Summary and Primer for Acting
on What We Have Learned

"IDEAS ARE NOT ENOUGH. Do our ideals fail because we do not know whether to believe in them? No. Our ideals fail because we do not know how to live them."[1]

> Bil: I don't have any hands to hold the instructions//where are the instructions?
>
> It's okay.
> Building trust can sometimes feel like making the Mona Lisa with two non-dominant hands and an Etcha-Sketch.
>   love and no B.S.
>   K.D.[2]

Faith communities can be places where people know they matter. Regardless. Without questions or conditions. They can be places where people can breathe. They can be places where people can find sanctuary. Not all faith communities are these things. Yet. But we can be. The world is mended not always through big sweeping events, but through the small acts of people living with courage in day to day ways of showing love to one another.

---

1. Welch, *Sweet Dreams*, 88.
2. Desimone, "I Don't Have Any Hands."

THE SPIRITUAL PRACTICE OF FEELING USELESS

It takes courage to hear and not look away. It takes courage to enter in, even if you don't know how you might have to change or even if you don't know what you can do to make things better. It's okay to feel a long way from where you want to be. But that's not an excuse not to do the work, even if it feels like you're working without all the tools you need.

In fact, in this work, it is sometimes good to feel what my wise friend Juan Carlos La Puente calls "the spiritual practice of feeling useless." It is this uselessness that turns up the need for us to simply listen, that quiets down our "fix it" jumping beans, and that allows us the opportunity to realize that we are awakening new possibilities together.

Juan Carlos continues, "If you feel your own vulnerability, then you will be open to your own transformation."[3] He cautions that in this process, the systems in our own hearts and minds might be in conflict with each other. The system of our mind that says, "Move. Fix. Hurry. You're supposed to be in charge here," will conflict with the system that says, "Slow down. Pay attention. Listen deeply. Follow another's lead." Many of us are not used to feeling useless. We are used to showing up and bringing something. We are taught if we have nothing to contribute maybe we shouldn't be there to begin with. But those notions perpetuate the systems causing our neighbors harm rather than challenging them. So, Juan Carlos reminds us, we have to be present before we can bring something. Feeling useless can teach us to be present, to make room for God to show up in unexpected ways, and for new possibilities to arise.

The communities highlighted in this book are not the only communities experiencing fear and pressure in our time. Indigenous communities, women of color, people with disabilities, and survivors of sexual assault are among other communities we need to listen to deeply. This list is not exhaustive. We live in the age of #MeToo and #BlackLivesMatter. We live in an age of a flurry of firings for inappropriate behaviors that have become public, inappropriate comments that get tweeted out. Some might think it is about time. Some might think some of this is overreaction. Yes, we often need to ask critical questions in each situation, but this is also calling us to be better. As Juan Carlos reminded us early in this book, there are people suffering our learning. Some of our learning processes hurt. Some of those

3. La Puente and Werner, "Organizing for Social Change."

suffering them are saying, "enough." We need to get better quicker. But not always in the ways that we assume.

Our neighbors in this book have offered us numerous gifts to help us along our way. They offer us frameworks for doing the work of love and doing it in ways that they receive as love. If we skinny them down to the basics, they are telling us: Listen (and shut up for a minute). Show up. Do your own work. Realize when it is about you and when it isn't. Accept non-closure. Then, provide the practical care that you hear us ask for in the ways you hear us ask for it.

These are essential components. They are also in an important order. Some of us want to jump to the practical care before we have paused to listen to what kind of care our neighbors actually want and need. That likely will serve more to soothe our own aching consciences rather than meet the needs of our neighbors. Some of us want to spend our whole lives listening and never move to acting. That might remove some aloneness in important moments, but leave our neighbors feeling exposed and alone in others. Some of us want to show up to drop off and then go home. That may provide some material goods that are needed but does not demonstrate what our neighbors consider love.

For love to be received as love, it is practical, it attends to larger structures, and it requires the possibility of relationship not determined by power dynamics. It requires the possibility of mutual exchange that may create different conditions for both of us. It requires opportunities to listen and learn and act to make life more bearable and life-giving together. We might have to feel useless for a little while as we learn what this means.

THE SPIRITUAL PRACTICES OF LISTENING AND SHOWING UP

One way to think about this process of offering love that is received as love is through the categories that my friends Juan Carlos and Ron offer in what they call, "Sacramental Organizing." In using the term "sacramental," Ron and Juan Carlos reinforce that every action can be an act of communicating grace in the world. Every action can be an act of reminding us of our roots and our vision that we long for and work toward. Every action can also be an opportunity to enact and experience a sliver of the world we hope for and toward which we work in real time. We may not usher the entire kin-dom of God in at once, but we can model it in our actions with each other in small and large ways. We can point to what we imagine. In that, each action also opens up our collective imaginations and brings new possibilities into our midst. Everyday acts of sacrament can become "truthful actions," actions that challenge the ways we often think about what it means and by what processes we can make change in our neighborhoods and world. This sets a different tone. It also sometimes sets a different pace.

Drawing on the work of Paulo Freire,[4] Raimon Panikkar,[5] and others, Ron and Juan Carlos remind us that this is a process and, in it, there is a "path to get into a deeper relationship and truthful ground in which our hearts together with our neighbors could imagine new possibilities and new practices to be used for social change." It does not produce a loving process for us to jump into someone else's reality and begin telling everyone what to do. We need to experience being a spectator and being present before we can begin to be a character in the story. And it is only over time that the possibilities open up for us to be co-authors together with our neighbors in what will become our shared future.[6]

In the stage of being a spectator, we have the opportunity and the responsibility to open our eyes to our neighborhoods and our worlds, to de-center ourselves from the role of major players, and to take the role of observer of what is going on around us. In this stage, we are practicing what it is to observe and listen as our neighbors throughout this text have reminded us. We are opening our ears, our minds, and our hearts to what is. We are beginning to pay attention to what gets our attention and theirs.

This creates an opportunity for us to identify who our neighbors are and where our neighbors are gathering to discuss things that are important to them and can become important to us. It creates an opportunity for us to practice what my friend Richard Twiss used to call "the theology of showing up." It creates an opportunity for us to be present in those spaces and conversations. It creates an opportunity for us to listen and learn.

If you are hearing concerning things about the experiences of Muslims in your community, find out when the Muslim community will be gathering for a community conversation. Contact someone to see if the gathering is open to the neighborhood. Then, if it is, show up and listen.

4. See Freire, *Pedagogy of the Oppressed*.

5. See Panikkar, *Invisible Harmony*.

6. Conversation with La Puente and Werner reflecting on the workshop "Organizing for Social Change."

If you are concerned about bullying in schools or online, find out when the Parent Teacher Association or school board meets for your local schools. Show up. Listen to what is shared about the realities surrounding these concerns.

If you are experiencing conflict between the calls in your sacred text to welcome the stranger and the messages you hear about immigrants in our community, find out if there are any immigrant led organizations nearby. Find out when they meet. Contact someone to see if the gathering is open to the public. If it is, show up and listen.

Show up. Show up again. Show up again. In some of these spaces, people may ask you why you are there. Be prepared to answer your why. Why did you want to show up? As Juan Carlos and Ron remind us, leave your credentials and agenda at the door. Answer the question of why you showed up honestly and from your heart, at the human to human level, not at your job or role in your faith community level.

In some of these environments, you may be an outsider. Realize the kind of weight that carries and the anxieties that it may hold for others in the room. You may be asked to justify your presence in stronger terms. In these moments, it is even more important to speak from your heart. Posturing your credentials or hiding behind an organization will likely not help. Humility and humanity has a better chance. Don't force yourself into any closed meeting. For those that are open, come wanting to listen and learn. It is both that simple and that difficult.

In showing up and showing up again and showing up again, your neighbors will begin to see you. They will see you showing up. They will see you learning with interest and honesty and vulnerability. That pattern is what will re-credential you as someone who may have the opportunity to speak and contribute ideas. That process also might take months.

THE SPIRITUAL PRACTICE OF DOING OUR OWN HOMEWORK

Throughout these first two stages, our neighbors in this book consistently ask that we please continue to do our own homework. As we listen, as we observe, they ask that we identify what our questions are and do the work of researching answers to those questions. They encourage us to pay attention to moments when we feel uncomfortable, to flag those, and then to dig deep into the causes of that discomfort. They encourage us to continue to discern when something is about us and when it actually isn't about us at all and to not make ourselves the center of something that isn't really about us.

This is hard work. It is also our work to do. Love requires relationship. It often requires mutuality and if one partner does not do their own work, that mutuality is jeopardized.

In our process, we may hear or experience things that cause us to weep and/or rage. Our neighbors remind us to not be afraid of big feelings but to resist becoming overwhelmed by guilt or uselessness. Learn from our big feelings. Listen to them. Try to understand them. Do not let them become the outcome of the process. They are a teacher, not the goal. The goal is life abundant. The goal is love.

This process of learning how to love in ways that are received as love is not about proving that we are "good people" or not racist/sexist/homo-phobic/(fill in the blank). It is about knowing what life is like for each other, seeing how we're connected or disconnected, and having a fighting chance at love that actually feels like love and produces life in the world. Some of our ways of being might need to die in order for new ways to resurrect.

Ron quotes Parker Palmer in moments like this, saying, "When the going gets rough, turn to wonder."[7] When you hit sticky points or road-blocks, when you stumble onto big feelings, especially if they surprise you, flag those. Turn to those with curiosity and ask yourself: Why is this hitting me in these ways? Why do I feel so strongly about this? Dig into your own stories and your own wells. Be vulnerable and honest with yourself. For that is not weakness, but strength in this process.

The practice of doing your own homework never really ends but there comes a time as you continue to do the work and continue to show up, when you will have earned the opportunity to speak. This is when, in Juan Carlos's and Ron's language, you can begin to be a character in the story. You can begin to ask questions. You can begin to make suggestions. You can begin to take leadership of certain components and make connections between people and concerns. But you are still not in charge. Those you are learning to love are the ones in charge. Those who are most impacted by the concerns in the room are the ones in charge. You are learning to be a good partner to them.

---

7. This is one of the Circle of Trust Touchstones for the Center for Courage & Renewal founded by Parker J. Palmer. You can read the touchstones here: *http://www.couragerenewal.org/touchstones/*.

And, when invited, you may also eventually become a co-author of actions and responses to the pressures that your neighbors experience in the world, of a new way of being together, of a model of being neighbors in the midst of messages telling us that we should be afraid of one another. These actions, if produced out of a process of deep listening and working together, will have a better chance of meeting real need, empowering those needing empowered, and feeling like love. When we know each other, we can love each other in ways that count. We are also less likely to be afraid of one another.

THE SPIRITUAL PRACTICE OF RISK

There are risks and learnings at each of these stages. There is the risk of showing up in a space where we are not welcome or where our presence inhibits the environment for others. There is a risk of speaking before we have established the credibility to do so. There is a risk of saying or doing the wrong thing at the wrong time. There is the risk of not saying or not doing the right thing at the right time.

There is also the risk of being associated with "those people" which may bring rejection to you as it has to our neighbors. In this era, being a welcoming community for those who are different may take a political nature to it. Exclusion of some groups has become synonymous with particular party lines and/or political stances. It has sometimes been synonymous with certain religious beliefs as well. To actively and compassionately engage the communities highlighted in this text might raise some eyebrows or blood pressure in some communities. It might bring downright rejection. That doesn't mean it is the wrong thing to do. Jesus raised a lot of eyebrows, too. We will be in good company.

And with all of these risks, fear may begin to raise its rascally little head again. Only we don't have to let it have control. We can choose to not shrink back to avoid risk. We can choose to not strike first to protect ourselves from getting hurt. When fear and anxiety do show up, we can notice them. We can name them. We can invite them to have a seat, we can explore where they came from, and we can take a breath and continue to listen to our neighbors and continue to seek courage. We can remind our fear and ourselves along the way that the risks we are taking are far less risky than the risk of doing nothing at all.

THE SPIRITUAL PRACTICE OF DOING AND BEING: LOVE AS A WHAT AND A HOW

In my classes, as I am helping my students to learn methods of engaging their communities to make helpful social change, I remind them (and myself) often, that love is as much a how as it is a what. It is a way as much as it is a feeling or experience. We have heard that throughout this book. Yes, we are concerned with outcomes. We are concerned that people know we love them and we are concerned that the ways we show them that love are concrete and connect with them in the ways that they feel that love. This is one of our goals.

It is also possible that we can offer the same things in a way that simply does not feel like love. We have heard this throughout the book as well. The things we offer are not the love in and of themselves. Love is produced in the way those gifts are offered, in the relationship out of which they are offered, with the humanizing dignity the act of care produces in both parties.

I ask my students, as we go through our process, whether they are planning a meeting or preparing for a type of social action to think: What kinds of things can we do, what kind of environment can we build, what kind of people can we be that will communicate care to people from the moment they arrive until the moment they leave us? Love is something that we produce in the world. It is also the way we are with one another. It is a "what." It is also a "how."

Faith communities have an opportunity to be something different than what we see modeled elsewhere. We can say yes to love, even of our enemies. In fact, we are called to. We can say no to fear that is excessive or misplaced. We have the opportunity to do the pre-figurative and sacramental work of dreaming up the world we long for, the world we think God dreams about, the world when all will be well for all people, the world that God is drawing us toward. How does that world want us to act? How might we inch our way toward becoming that right now, so that others, too, can see and experience that vision?

THE SPIRITUAL PRACTICE OF ACCEPTING NON-CLOSURE.

The world we have inherited does not have to be the world we leave behind. But it is the world we have now. The last piece of advice that our neighbors have offered us in this book, often implicitly, is to accept non-closure. In our process of honestly listening and learning, of showing up and showing up and showing up again, of doing our own homework and recognizing our places of big feelings and questions, of earning the right to speak and support, of discerning through that process of intentional engagement what actually feels like love to our real neighbors (not simply our perceptions of who they might be), and offering that practical (both personalized and structural) love, we know that our work is still not done. This is not something that can be checked off of a list.

Sometimes we will still miss. Sometimes the needs are greater than we expected. Sometimes we will be misunderstood or unwanted or asked to leave because we, too, carry more than our individual selves. Sometimes we represent power structures and systemic dynamics that trigger people's experiences of harm. In those moments, we remember again that it is not about us. Except for when it is. We circle back and continue to do our own homework. We circle back and continue, with honesty and humility, to listen and learn. We offer prayers of gratitude to and for our neighbors who have been our patient (and sometimes not-so-patient) teachers along the way. We offer prayers for forgiveness to our neighbors when we continue to cause harm because we said or did the wrong thing or didn't say or do the right thing. We celebrate the little and sometimes big "wins" of learning and discovering along the way and the relationships that form.

As faith communities, sometimes we get too concerned about who will enjoy the afterlife that we forget to be wholeheartedly concerned with who feels welcome in our presence now. There have been many moments in the history of the Christian faith when Jesus-followers had to make significant decisions about who they were going to be. The Jerusalem council in Acts 15 decided to lift former restrictions and find a way for Gentiles to join the community. They declared: Let us not give them any unnecessary burdens to follow Jesus. The post-persecution era church wrestled with whether or not to let people back in who ran away during persecution. They asked: Will we hold the line and be identified primarily as a community of purity demonstrated in familiar ways or will we be primarily identified as a community of open and forgiving love to those who ran away? Often, our ancestors have tried to have and be both. Sometimes that has led to having neither. We, too, make these kinds of decisions in big and small ways all the time. In making love central, in following the way of Jesus, where is our love too small or too narrow? Where do we hold to unnecessary burdens? This work is constant.

Accepting non-closure is part of the deal. We will likely walk out of some conversations and moments feeling very unsettled and unsatisfied. Things don't tie up in neat little bows very often. We cannot predict every timeline. Soothing our hurt feelings is not always a top priority. That has to be okay. That is part of our work. We don't do it alone but we still have to do it.

So we keep working. Because the work isn't done. Because all is not yet well with everyone. Because we can no longer not do something. And because, as my friend Lolly says, reminding someone that they are beloved "seems to be about the best thing one human can do for another."[8] There is joy in this struggle that leads to love. And although we may feel sometimes like we don't have all the tools, we may be surprised to find that we have everything we need.

So, to my fellow beloved lovers living in this time of fear: may the God who created both the living and the dead, the settled and the sojourner, the comforted and the hurting, the God who accompanies us on the sometimes long and dusty road, who can breathe life into even the driest of bones, who shows up in the midst of the fiery flames, may this God remove our aloneness, grant us hope, and give us courage. There is enough. And I'm glad you're here.

8. Bargerstock, Facebook.

Appendix

(Not) The End

Tools for the Journey

THIS BOOK IS SIMPLY a beginning. Here are a few tools to help you further the work:

LOVE IN A TIME OF FEAR TOOLKIT FOR GROUPS

At www.loveinatimeoffear.com you will find a guide for using this book and the *Love in a Time of Fear* documentary short films with groups. This toolkit is designed with faith communities or neighborhood groups in mind to process what you are learning together.

PROJECT IMPLICIT, EXPLORING IMPLICIT ASSOCIATIONS

Several times throughout the book I mentioned the notion of implicit biases. At https://implicit.harvard.edu/implicit you can take several tests to measure your implicit social attitudes regarding religion, race, age, disability, sexuality, weight, gender, and other topics. These tools are helpful to understand what sometimes goes on at a subconscious level so that you can be aware of how you might be responding in ways that feel contradictory to your values and so that you can be aware of areas that you may want to continue to intentionally address on the journey toward care for all people.

AGREEMENTS FOR "COURAGEOUS CONVERSATIONS"

When engaging potentially divisive or charged conversations, it may be helpful to keep in mind the "Agreements for Courageous Conversations and Active Learning." Those agreements echo what our neighbors shared throughout the book and are:

- Stay Engaged
- Experience Discomfort
- Speak Your Truth
- Expect and Accept Non-Closure
- Maintain Confidentiality
- Listen with the Intent to Learn
- Suspend Judgment.[1]

TIPS FOR HAVING 1 TO 1 CONVERSATIONS

After you have already spent some time showing up and listening deeply, you may want to follow up with particular people for a "1 to 1" conversation. This is not an interview but a somewhat short (typically 30–45 minutes), mutual, curious conversation to learn more about what you have been hearing and with an ear toward places where you might learn more or work together to create helpful change.

- Before meeting, consider what you already know about the person. What are you curious about? To what do you need to be potentially sensitive? Consider what brought you into the conversation. What connects you to the person? Why are you curious to learn more?

- In the conversation itself, listen both to what is being said and what is not being said.

- Remember this is not an interview. Be reciprocal. Offer parts of your story and experiences as they connect to your partner's to match and model vulnerability.

1. These can be found several places. One of those is http://www.nonprofitinclusiveness.org/agreements-courageous-conversations-and-active-learning.

- Ask questions that draw out rather than shut down the conversation. For example: Ask about why your conversation partner is involved in the issues that brought you together. Share your story of why. Ask about their passions or hopes. Ask about the pressures they or their family members experience. Keep listening for stories and for their "why."

- Respect their time and presence and be sure to end when you said you were going to end. Accept non-closure. After the conversation, write down what seemed to be the major questions or themes they expressed or were underneath what they said. Write down the questions you want to know more about. Then, consider doing more research on your own or invite them for another conversation.[2]

A MODEL FOR GUIDED GROUP CONVERSATIONS REGARDING DIFFICULT TOPICS

If you want to invite someone to help facilitate a conversation about difficult things in our nation today, check out Michelle Lang and The Art of Tough Talks: http://www.theartoftoughtalks.com.

If you are facilitating conversations yourself, consider using the following as guidelines in a small group conversation about potentially divisive topics.[3]

- Focus on the simple questions: What are my hopes, fears, and/or personal experiences regarding (the day's issue)? Stick to those questions. This keeps it personal rather than theoretical or from hearsay.

- Do not be afraid of silence. Do not rush to fill the space.

- Do not be afraid to speak. Encourage each person to share.

- Do not feel pressured to speak every time. You can participate fully by listening attentively but do not withhold your thoughts from the group.

- When you speak, speak carefully and make space for others. Be mindful of how long you speak. Do not share a second time until others have all had the opportunity to share.

2. Adapted from IAF Northwest materials on "Best Practices for Individual Relational Meetings."

3. Adapted from the Quaker practice of and guidelines for Worship Sharing.

- Listen fully to each other. Do not interrupt someone else. Do not be afraid to allow space for silence between group members' sharings in order that all might consider what has just been said for a moment before moving to the next speaker. Hold the gift the person just offered with respect.

- Speak from your experience not from the experiences only of others or abstract theories you do not experientially understand. Focus primarily on direct experiences and avoid a "back and forth" or a debate with what your group-mates have just shared. That may be for another time after you have had a chance to really listen to each other first.

- Respect each other and the conversation. If what is shared is personal, do not share it outside of the conversation unless the person who shared it gives permission.

THREE PRACTICES TO USE WHEN FEELING OVERWHELMED

- Breathe. Sometimes when anxiety or overwhelm hits, we forget to breathe. Taking a moment to intentionally breathe deeply can help calm feelings of overwhelm.

- Follow the "3–3–3 Rule." When you feel your brain "going 100 miles per hour," look around and identify and name three things that you see. Then turn to another of your senses and identify and name three sounds you hear. After that, recognize what is going on in your body and slowly move three body parts. Wriggle your fingers, lift your foot, twirl your ankle. In high stress moments, "this mental trick can help center your mind, bringing you back to the present moment."[4]

- Stand up straight. "When we are anxious, we protect our upper body—where our heart and lungs are located—by hunching over." In order to address this in any given moment, "pull your shoulders back, stand or sit with your feet apart, and open your chest. This helps your body start to sense that it's back in control."[5]

4. Hughes, "How to Stop Feeling Anxious."
5. Ibid.

These are only three. There are many practices for addressing anxiety or feelings of overwhelm. Explore the ones that work for you.

A NON-EXHAUSTIVE LIST OF FILMS AND BOOKS TO READ AND WATCH TO LEARN MORE[6]

On Immigrant Experience in the US

Films

Made in L.A. (2007)

Sin Pais (2010, http://inationmedia.com/sinpais)

Limbo (2012, https://vimeo.com/35672609)

Documented (2013)

No Le Digas A Nadie/Don't Tell Anyone (2015)

Books

Trails of Hope and Terror: Testimonies on Immigration by Miguel A. De La Torre

The US Immigration Crisis: Toward an Ethics of Place by Miguel A. De La Torre

The Book of Unknown Americans, a novel, by Cristina Henríquez

Tell Me How It Ends: An Essay in 40 Questions by Valeria Luiselli

On Muslim Experience in the US

Films

The Visitor (2007)

America at a Crossroads: The Muslim Americans (PBS, 2007)

Allah Made Me Funny (2008)

New Muslim Cool (2009)

---

6. For each category, also consider doing google searches for "must read/watch" books and film lists.

Books

Living Islam Out Loud: American Muslim Women Speak edited by Saleemah Abdul-Ghafur

This Muslim American Life: Dispatches from the War on Terror by Moustafa Bayoumi

Acts of Faith: The Story of an American Muslim, the Struggle for the Soul of a Generation by Eboo Patel

Demystifying Islam: Tackling the Tough Questions by Harris Zafar

On LGBTQ+ Experience

Films

Gayby Baby (2015)

Freedom to Marry (2016)

Gender Revolution (2017)

The new *Queer Eye,* Season 2, Episode 1 (2018)

Books

Changing Our Mind by David Gushee

Rescuing Jesus: How People of Color, Women, and Queer Christians are Reclaiming Evangelicalism by Deborah Jian Lee

UnClobber: Rethinking Our Misuse of the Bible on Homosexuality by Colby Martin

Everything written by Pádraig Ó Tuama, especially the papers, "Love is the Great Endeavour," "Welcoming the Neighbour," and "Holding the Tension Wisely," found in their entirety at: http://www.padraigotuama.com/writing

Our Witness: The Unheard Stories of LGBT+ Christians edited by Brandan Robertson

On African American Experience

Films

Boyz N The Hood (1991)

Lalee's Kin (2001)

Freedom Riders (2010)

The 13th (2016)

The African Americans: Many Rivers to Cross (http://www.pbs.org/wnet/african-americans-many-rivers-to-cross)

Books

I'm Still Here: Black Dignity in a World Made for Whiteness by Austin Channing Brown

Between the World and Me by Ta-Nehisi Coates

The Cross and the Lynching Tree by James H. Cone

Ferguson & Faith: Sparking Leadership & Awakening Community by Leah Gunning Francis

The Guitar Section: A Sound Check on Justice, a short play by Michelle Lang

America's Original Sin: Racism, White Privilege, and the Bridge to a New America by Jim Wallis or *The Myth of Equality: Uncovering the Roots of Injustice and Privilege* by Ken Wytsma

Acknowledgments

To HEAR AND TO hold the stories unfolded in this book and its accompanying films has been a heartbreaking, heart-filling, and inspiring gift. I know that I have been witness and participant in something sacred here. I have a lot of thanks to give.

To those of you who offered your stories as a gift to us all—Erendira, Andy, Montse, Blanca, Nelly, Veronica, Victor, Gimena, Arman, Nairyna, Sahar, Nasreen, Sameya, Almir, Harris, Kori, Shayla, Sarah, Beth, John, Alaine, Isaac, Josh, Deborah, Da'Lorian, Montel, Ryan, Fernando, Hakeem, and Josh—thank you for your courage and honesty. Thank you for trusting me to help tell your stories. This book is for you.

Thank you to Sebastian and Peripheral Vision PDX for the heart and soul, time and grit you put into making beautiful documentary portraits to help the stories in this book come alive. (And an extra thank you to your family who shared you. Theirs, too, was a gift of love.)

Thank you to the many people who read chapters, viewed films, and/or offered timely and crucial thoughts along the way: Michelle, Arthur, Serena, Morgan, Collin, Pete, Kia, Juan Carlos, Ron, Sebastian, Jeanie, JR, Leroy, Harris, Charlie, Jennifer, Sarah, and Stacia. Your voices are in here. You make this project better.

Thank you to the good people at Wipf & Stock who worked diligently on taking this project from concept to finish. It has been an honor (and breeze) to work with you.

Thank you to the good people at Warner Pacific University for having the heart and the courage to begin making an environment that brings some of the best students on the planet together, where conversations like these can take place, where fruitful learning happens that can still change the world. We are not yet what we will become. But magic happens every day and I am so grateful to be a part of it.

Acknowledgments

Thank you to my neighbors in Kansas, Indiana, Chicago, Uganda, and Portland. You have been my teachers.

Thank you to my deep support system, to friends who inquired, who checked in, who enlivened, who believed, who make life full and joyful: Serena, Michelle, Jess, Robin, Luke, Jessie, Carolyn, Kyra, Jeanie, Derek, Terry, Melissa, Ron, Juan Carlos, Chris, Beth, Jarod, Jennifer, Kelly, Stephanie, to my friends in the Interfaith Movement for Immigrant Justice, the Interfaith Council of Greater Portland, and the lively and joyful community of faith leaders who have become my people and made me their own.

And to my family, my extended family who hold us all together, my parents who believe in me and what I do, even when it is like pulling teeth to get information out of me. And to Perry, Winston, and Gretchen: you are my heartbeats. I offer and credit all that I am and all that I hope to be to you. Thank you, my loves.

Bibliography

All Things Considered. "Millions Raised for Immigrants Will Be Used to Provide Legal Support." NPR, June 21, 2018.

Bader-Saye, Scott. *Following Jesus in a Culture of Fear*. Grand Rapids, MI: Press, 2007.

Baldwin, James. "A Talk to Teachers." Originally published in *The Saturday Review*, December 21, 1963, reprinted in *The Price of the Ticket, Collected Non-Fiction 1948–1985*, New York: Saint Martin's, 1985.

Barber, Leroy. *Embrace: God's Radical Shalom for a Divided World*. Downers Grove, IL: IVP, 2016.

Bargerstock, Lolly. Facebook, May 20, 2017.

Barrett, Paul M. *American Islam: The Struggle for the Soul of a Religion*. New York: Picador, 2007.

Bayoumi, Moustafa. *This Muslim American Life: Dispatches From the War on Terror*. New York: New York University Press, 2015.

Bolz-Weber, Nadia. *Accidental Saints: Finding God in all the Wrong People*. New York: Convergent, 2015.

Bonhoeffer: Pastor, Pacifist, Nazi Resister. Directed by Martin Doblmeier. New York: First Run Features, 2003.

Brammer, John Paul. "Trump Reportedly Jokes About Mike Pence Wanting to 'Hang' Gays." *NBC News*, October 17, 2017. https://www.nbcnews.com/feature/nbc-out/trump-reportedly-jokes-about-mike-pence-wanting-hang-gays-n811086.

Brown, Austin Channing. *I'm Still Here: Black Dignity in a World Made for Whiteness*. New York: Convergent, 2018.

Brueggemann, Walter. *Peace*. Understanding Biblical Themes Series. St. Louis: Chalice, 2001.

Bump, Philip. "The Group Least Likely to Think the U.S. has a Responsibility to Accept Refugees? Evangelicals." *The Washington Post*, May 24, 2018. https://www.washingtonpost.com/news/politics/wp/2018/05/24/the-group-least-likely-to-think-the-u-s-has-a-responsibility-to-accept-refugees-evangelicals/?noredirect=on&utm_term=.cd43224585fd.

Burke, Daniel. "More Than 600 Members of Jeff Sessions' Church Just Charged Him with Violating Church Rules." CNN, June 19, 2018. https://www.cnn.com/2018/06/19/politics/sessions-church-complaint/index.html.

Cannon, Mae Elise, Lisa Sharon Harper, Troy Jackson, Soong-Chan Rah. *Forgive Us: Confessions of a Compromised Faith*. Grand Rapids, MI: Zondervan, 2014.

Center for Courage & Renewal. "Circle of Trust Touchstones." Accessed June 1, 2018. http://www.couragerenewal.org/touchstones/.

Chapman University, "America's Top Fears 2017: Chapman University Survey of American Fears." Posted October 11, 2017. https://blogs.chapman.edu/wilkinson/2017/10/11/americas-top-fears-2017/.

Coates, Ta-Nehisi. *Between the World and Me.* New York: Spiegel & Grau: New York, 2015.

Davis, Julie Hirschfeld, Sheryl Gay Stolberg, and Thomas Kaplan. "Trump Alarms Lawmakers With Disparaging Words for Haiti and Africa." *The New York Times,* January 11, 2018. https://www.nytimes.com/2018/01/11/us/politics/trump-shithole-countries.html.

De La Torre, Miguel A. "For Immigrants." In *To Do Justice: A Guide for Progressive Christians,* edited by Rebecca Todd Peters and Elizabeth Hinson-Hasty, 73–84. Louisville, KY: Westminster John Knox, 2008.

———. *Trails of Hope and Terror: Testimonies on Immigration.* Maryknoll, NY: Orbis, 20009.

The Denver Foundation. "Agreements for Courageous Conversations and Active Learning." Accessed June 8, 2018. http://www.nonprofitinclusiveness.org/agreements-courageous-conversations-and-active-learning.

DeSimone, Kori. "How Do We Each Name Something We're all Experiencing?" Instagram for love.and.no.bs, November 21, 2017.

———. "I Don't Have Any Hands to Hold the Instructions//Where Are the Instructions?" Instagram for love.and.no.bs, September 14, 2017.

———. "On Where I Am Theologically." Instagram for love.and.no.bs, September 23, 2017.

Eiser, Peter. "Trump Won With Lowest Minority Vote in Decades, Fueling Divisions," *Reuters,* November 23, 2016. https://www.reuters.com/article/us-usa-trump-polarization-analysis/trump-won-with-lowest-minority-vote-in-decades-fueling-divisions-idUSKBN13I10B.

Freire, Paulo. *Pedagogy of the Oppressed.* Translated by Myra Bergman Ramos. 1970. Reprint. New York: Continuum, 1999.

God in America: How Religious Liberty Shaped America. Directed by David Belton. Boston: WGBH, 2010. http://www.pbs.org/godinamerica/view/.

Gushee, David P. *Changing Our Mind: Definitive 3rd Edition of the Landmark Call for Inclusion of LGBTQ Christians with Response to Critics.* Canton, MI: Read The Spirit Books, 2017.

Haas, Ann P., Philip L. Rodgers, and Jody L. Herman, "Suicide Attempts Among Transgender and Gender Non-Conforming Adults." American Foundation for Suicide Prevention and the Williams Institute on Sexual Orientation and Gender Identity Law and Public Policy at UCLA School of Law, January 2014. http://williamsinstitute.law.ucla.edu/wp-content/uploads/AFSP-Williams-Suicide-Report-Final.pdf.

Hanson, Elise. "The Forgotten Minority in Police Shootings," CNN, November 13, 2017. https://www.cnn.com/2017/11/10/us/native-lives-matter/index.html.

Harper, Lisa Sharon. *The Very Good Gospel: How Everything Wrong Can Be Made Right.* New York: Waterbrook, 2016.

Hatzenbuehler, Mark L. et al. "Effects of Same-Sex Marriage Laws on Health Care Use and Expenditures in Sexual Minority Men: A Quasi-Natural Experiment." In *American Journal of Public Health* 102 2 (2012).

Hoffman, Gene Knudsen. "An Enemy is One Whose Story We Have Not Heard." *Fellowship, the Journal of the Fellowship of Reconciliation* (May/June 1997). https://www.newconversations.net/communication-skills-library-of-articles-and-teaching-materials/gene-knudsen-hoffman-articles/an-enemy-is-one-whose-story-we-have-not-heard/.

Holson, Laura M. "Hundred in Oakland Turn Out to BBQ While Black." *The New York Times,* May 21, 2018. https://www.nytimes.com/2018/05/21/us/oakland-bbq-while-black.html.

Hughes, Locke. "How to Stop Feeling Anxious Right Now." *WebMD.* Accessed June 1, 2018. https://www.webmd.com/mental-health/features/ways-to-reduce-anxiety.

Human Rights Campaign. "National Coming Out Day Youth Report." Accessed June 11, 2018. https://assets2.hrc.org/files/assets/resources/NCOD-Youth-Report.pdf?_ga=2.240544006.448810262.1520029389-648005722.1520029389.

———. "Policy and Position Statements on Conversion Therapy." Accessed June 1, 2018. https://www.hrc.org/resources/policy-and-position-statements-on-conversion-therapy.

Information is Beautiful. "Rhetological Fallacies: Errors and Manipulation of Rhetoric and Logical Thinking." Accessed June 18, 2018. https://informationisbeautiful.net/visualizations/rhetological-fallacies.

Isasi-Díaz, Ada María. *La Lucha Continues: Mujerista Theology.* Maryknoll, NY: Orbis, 2004.

Kann, Laura et al. "Sexual Identity, Sex of Sexual Contacts, and Health-Risk Behaviors Among Students in Grades 9–12." Centers for Disease Control and Prevention, June 6, 2011. http://www.cdc.gov/mmwr/pdf/ss/ss60e0606.pdf.

Khimm, Suzy. "How Long is the Immigration 'Line'? As Long as 24 Years." *The Washington Post,* January 31, 2013. https://www.washingtonpost.com/news/wonk/wp/2013/01/31/how-long-is-the-immigration-line-as-long-as-24-years/?utm_term=.373a6038017/.

King, Martin Luther, Jr. "Letter from Birmingham City Jail." In *A Testament of Hope: The Essential Writings and Speeches of Martin Luther King, Jr,* edited by James M. Washington, 289–302. New York: HarperSanFrancisco, 1986.

Kuruvilla, Carol. "Chilling Study Sums Up Link Between Religion and Suicide for Queer Youth." *The Huffington Post,* April, 18, 2018. https://www.huffingtonpost.com/entry/queer-youth-religion-suicide-study_us_5ad4f7b3e4b077c89ceb9774.

La Puente, Juan Carlos and Ron Werner Jr., workshop on "Organizing for Social Change within the Ecclesia," and message to author, June 11, 2018.

Lee, Deborah Jian. *Rescuing Jesus: How People of Color, Women, & Queer Christians Are Reclaiming Evangelicalism.* Boston: Beacon, 2015.

Lipka, Michael. "How Many People of Different Faiths Do You Know?" *Pew Research Center,* July 17, 2014. http://www.pewresearch.org/fact-tank/2014/07/17/how-many-people-of-different-faiths-do-you-know/.

Martin, Colby. *UnClobber: Rethinking Our Misuse of the Bible on Homosexuality.* Louisville, KY: Westminster John Knox, 2016.

Martin, Fr. James, SJ. "Why Are We Having All These People from Sh#*hole Countries Come Here?" Facebook, January 12, 2018.

Matsushima, Paul. "The Struggles of Discussing Race in the Asian American Evangelical Church." In *Inheritance Magazine,* issue 60, May 2018. https://www.inheritancemag.

com/stories/the-struggles-of-discussing-race-in-the-asian-american-evangelical-church.

Miller, Emily McFarlan. "Austin Channing Brown: White People Are 'Exhausting.'" *Sojourners,* May 10, 2018. https://sojo.net/articles/austin-channing-brown-white-people-are-exhausting.

"The Missing." BBC video, 8:28. Posted by BBC, 15 Jan 2018. https://www.bbc.com/news/av/world-us-canada-42667659/the-missing-consequences-of-trump-s-immigration-crackdown.

Ó Tuama, Pádraig. "A Lived Theology of Listening." In *Holding the Tension Wisely,* a paper on the Irish Peace Center's Human Rights and Religious Ethics Working Conference, Ballycastle, County Antrim, Ireland, June 1–2, 2011. http://www.padraigotuama.com/writing/.

———. "Love is the Great Endeavor." Paper presented at The Church of Ireland Conference, March 29, 2014. http://www.padraigotuama.com/blog/loveisthegreatendeavour.

———. "Love is the Great Endeavor—Audio and Text from C of I Conf, March 29, 2014." In the shelter (blog), March 30, 2014. http://www.padraigotuama.com/blog/loveisthegreatendeavour.

———. "Welcoming the Neighbor." Presentation at the launch of Changing Attitude Ireland's Parish Welcoming Leaflet, Belfast, Ireland, May 17, 2012. http://www.padraigotuama.com/writing/.

Oxford Dictionaries. "Defining 'White Fragility.'" Accessed June 8, 2018. https://blog.oxforddictionaries.com/2017/12/15/white-fragility-word-of-the-year-2017-shortlist/.

Panikkar, Raimon. *Invisible Harmony.* Minneapolis: Fortress, 1995.

"Protest at Ahmadiyya Muslim Community Rizwan Mosque, Portland, Oregon." You Tube video, 1:22. Posted by Ismat Sarah Mangla, Nov 15, 2015. https://www.youtube.com/watch?v=w1ZypJ1hINo.

Rukeyser, Muriel. "Kathe Kollwitz." In *The Collected Poems of Muriel Rukeyser,* edited by Janet E. Kaufman and Anne F. Herzog, 460–64. Pittsburgh, PA: University of Pittsburgh Press, 2005.

Smith, Clint. "How to Raise a Black Son in America." TED Talk video, 5:13. Posted by TED Talks, March 2015. https://www.ted.com/talks/clint_smith_how_to_raise_a_black_son_in_america.

Smith, Gregory A., and Jessica Martínez. "How the Faithful Voted: A Preliminary 2016 Analysis." *Pew Research Center,* November 9, 2016. http://www.pewresearch.org/fact-tank/2016/11/09/how-the-faithful-voted-a-preliminary-2016-analysis/.

Smith, Mitzi J. *Womanist Sass and Talk Back: Social (In)Justice, Intersectionality, and Biblical Interpretation.* Eugene, OR: Cascade, 2018.

Trentaz, Cassie J. E. H. "'In the City, for the City': Re-Membering Roots and Discovering What it Means to be Our Full Selves and Good Neighbors in Southeast Portland." In *Holy Imagination: Rethinking Social Holiness,* edited by Nathan Crawford, Jonathan Dodrill, and David Wilson, 161–74. Lexington, KY: Emeth, 2015.

———. *Theology in the Age of AIDS & HIV: Complicity and Possibility.* New York: Palgrave Macmillan, 2012.

U.S. Citizenship and Immigration Services. "Consideration of Deferred Action for Childhood Arrivals (DACA)." Accessed May 25, 2018. https://www.uscis.gov/archive/consideration-deferred-action-childhood-arrivals-daca.

Wallace, David Foster. *This is Water: Some Thoughts, Delivered on a Significant Occasion, about Living a Compassionate Life*. New York: Little, Brown and Company, 2009.

Wallis, Jim. *America's Original Sin: Racism, White Privilege, and the Bridge to a New America*. Grand Rapids, MI: Brazos, 2016.

Welch, Sharon D. *Sweet Dreams in America: Making Ethics and Spirituality Work*. New York: Routledge, 1999.

Williams, Paula Stone. "I've Lived as a Man & a Woman—Here's What I Learned." *TEDxMileHigh* video, 15:24. Posted by TEDx Talks on Dec 19, 2017. https://www.youtube.com/watch?v=lrYx7HaUlMY.

Wilson, Conrad. "Detainees in Oregon Say They Followed Asylum Process and Were Arrested." OPB, June 19, 2018. https://www.opb.org/news/article/oregon-prison-asylum-zero-tolerance-immigration-children/.

Wytsma, Ken. *The Myth of Equality: Uncovering the Roots of Injustice and Privilege*. Downers Grover, IL: InterVarsity, 2017.

Zafar, Harris. "Demystifying 'the Other.'" TEDxSpeedwayPlaza video, 14:14. Posted by TEDx Talks, Nov 17, 2014. https://www.youtube.com/watch?v=rrgae7d6iI4.

59488962R00096

Made in the USA
Columbia, SC
04 June 2019